THE
PRAYER
OF
PROTECTION

ALSO BY JOSEPH PRINCE

Reign in Life

The Power of Right Believing

100 Days of Right Believing

Grace Revolution

Glorious Grace

Destined To Reign

Unmerited Favor

100 Days of Favor

Healing Promises

Provision Promises

Health And Wholeness Through The Holy Communion

A Life Worth Living

The Benjamin Generation

Your Miracle Is In Your Mouth

Right Place Right Time

Spiritual Warfare

For more information on these books and other inspiring resources,
visit JosephPrince.com.

JOSEPH PRINCE

THE
PRAYER
OF
PROTECTION

LIVING FEARLESSLY IN DANGEROUS TIMES

FaithWords

New York · Nashville

FaithWords
Hachette Book Group
1290 Avenue of the Americas, New York, NY 10104
faithwords.com
twitter.com/faithwords

Originally published in hardcover and ebook by FaithWords in November 2016.
First Trade Paperback Edition: September 2017

FaithWords is a division of Hachette Book Group, Inc. The FaithWords name and logo are trademarks of Hachette Book Group, Inc.

The publisher is not responsible for websites (or their content) that are not owned by the publisher.

The Hachette Speakers Bureau provides a wide range of authors for speaking events. To find out more, go to www.hachettespeakersbureau.com or call (866) 376-6591.

Library of Congress Cataloging-in-Publication Data

Names: Prince, Joseph, author.
Title: The prayer of protection : living fearlessly in dangerous times / Joseph Prince.
Description: First edition. | New York : FaithWords, [2016]
Identifiers: LCCN 2016025609 | ISBN 9781455569120 (hardcover) | ISBN 9781455542376 (large print) | ISBN 9781478912972 (audio download) | ISBN 9781478912965 (audio book) | ISBN 9781455569113 (ebook)
Subjects: LCSH: Bible. Psalms, XCI—Criticism, interpretation, etc.
Classification: LCC BS1450 91st .P75 2016 | DDC 248.4—dc23 LC record available at https://lccn.loc.gov/2016025609

ISBN: 978-1-4555-6912-0 (hardcover), 978-1-4555-4237-6 (hardcover large print), 978-1-4789-7085-9 (autographed edition), 978-1-4555-6913-7 (trade paperback), 978-1-4555-9837-3 (international trade paperback), 978-1-4555-6911-3 (ebook), 978-1-4789-4535-2 (South African paperback)

Printed in the United States of America

LSC-C

10   9   8   7   6   5   4   3   2

CONTENTS

INTRODUCTION

We live in dangerous times. A time in which a person could be attacked by terrorists while watching a concert. A time when a bomb could go off as someone sips on a latte in his favorite café. A time during which an epidemic from one country could spread to another through a single traveler. A time when earthquakes, floods, and other calamities seem to be happening all too often. A time of violence, conflict, and wars.

We can hardly get away from the constant bombardment of such negative news. It comes in through our newsfeeds. It turns up on social media. It screams at us from newspaper headlines and flashes across our screens as news outlets update us live on the senseless violence that wrecks so many lives.

My heart goes out to those whose lives have been devastated by hate-fueled attacks, as well as to those whose realities have been shaken in disasters beyond their control.

Unfortunately, we already know that the world is going to get even darker.

Isaiah 60:2 tells us this:

> *Darkness shall cover the earth, and deep darkness the*
> *people.*

But I have good news for you, my friend. Good news of the promises in God's Word that will fortify you and equip you during these times. Good news of His protection and His favor upon you. Good news that declares that you are *in* this world, but not *of* this world!

Isaiah 60:2 does not end with deep darkness. It goes on to declare this:

> *But the* LORD *will arise over you, and His glory will be*
> *seen upon you.*

The darker the world becomes, the brighter YOU will shine. As gloom and despair cover the earth, your light will become increasingly radiant. You will be His beacon of grace and glory in the midst of deep darkness. The world will see you walking in the fullness of the Lord's blessings and favor, and wonder how you and your household could be protected from the destruction and chaos all around.

You may be familiar with the Old Testament story of Daniel's friends, who were thrown into a fiery furnace for refusing to bow down to the golden idol of King Nebuchadnezzar. The king, his governors, and his counselors all witnessed for themselves how the fire had no power over the three Hebrew boys. Not a single strand of their hair was singed nor were their garments scorched.

In fact, they walked away from the furnace without so much as the smell of smoke or fire on them!

Beloved, I want you to picture Daniel's friends walking out of that fiery furnace, completely unharmed. That's a picture of you and me today.

In Christ, we are in this world, but we are not of this world. Even when thrown into the most extreme and challenging circumstances, we can walk out unharmed.

The same Lord Jesus who stood with Shadrach, Meshach, and Abednego in the furnace stands with you today!

The darkness is real. The fire is real. The dangers in this world are certainly real, but His promise that you can live protected and untouched can be an even greater reality in your life.

That is why I wrote this book.

The Word of God tells us that fear involves torment. Our Father in heaven doesn't want any of His beloved children tormented by fear. His Word tells us, "There is no fear in love; but perfect love casts out fear" (1 John 4:18). I particularly like how the Amplified Bible says it:

> *There is no fear in love [dread does not exist], but full-grown (complete, perfect) love turns fear out of doors* and *expels every trace of terror!*

I wrote this book because I want you anchored in His protective love for you. I want *every* trace of fear to be expelled from your heart. Perhaps terrorism, wars, and calamities do not weigh your heart down, but fears of more immediate circumstances do. Fear of losing your job as rumors of retrenchments and job cuts travel through the grapevine. Fear that bodily symptoms you have been experiencing could develop into something sinister. Fear that your children could somehow get into trouble and be hurt.

Whatever fear it is that grips your heart, I have so much that I want to share with you that I know will garrison your heart. You are not a hapless bystander who has no choice but to live in fear. No, you are set apart by your heavenly Abba. You are His beloved, and He who watches over you *never* slumbers or sleeps (see Ps. 121:4)! And yet, we cannot take His protection for granted.

This is why I want to show you how you can pray the prayer of protection found in Psalm 91. Together, let us uncover what the Bible says about divine protection and learn faith-building truths that I know will strengthen you. I want you to be encouraged by amazing testimonies from people around the world who have experienced God's protection firsthand. Our Lord is the same yesterday, today, and forever. In the same way He supernaturally delivered the precious individuals whose stories you will get to read in this book, He will deliver you too. It is my prayer that as you journey through the powerful revelations contained in this book, you will be empowered to truly live confidently and fearlessly in these dangerous times.

THE PRAYER
OF PROTECTION

Psalm 91

He who dwells in the secret place of the Most High
Shall abide under the shadow of the Almighty.
2 I will say of the Lord, "He is my refuge and my fortress;
My God, in Him I will trust."

3 Surely He shall deliver you from the snare of the fowler
And from the perilous pestilence.
4 He shall cover you with His feathers,
And under His wings you shall take refuge;
His truth shall be your shield and buckler.
5 You shall not be afraid of the terror by night,
Nor of the arrow that flies by day,
6 Nor of the pestilence that walks in darkness,
Nor of the destruction that lays waste at noonday.

7 A thousand may fall at your side,
And ten thousand at your right hand;
But it shall not come near you.
8 Only with your eyes shall you look,
And see the reward of the wicked.

9 Because you have made the Lord, who is my refuge,
Even the Most High, your dwelling place,
10 No evil shall befall you,

Nor shall any plague come near your dwelling;
¹¹ For He shall give His angels charge over you,
To keep you in all your ways.
¹² In their *hands* they shall bear you up,
Lest you dash your foot against a stone.
¹³ You shall tread upon the lion and the cobra,
The young lion and the serpent you shall trample underfoot.

¹⁴ "Because he has set his love upon Me, therefore I will deliver him;
I will set him on high, because he has known My name.
¹⁵ He shall call upon Me, and I will answer him;
I will be *with him in trouble;*
I will deliver him and honor him.
¹⁶ With long life I will satisfy him,
And show him My salvation."

I
THE SECRET PLACE

He who dwells in the secret place of the Most High
Shall abide under the shadow of the Almighty.
—Psalm 91:1

There is a lot of fearmongering everywhere you turn today. On the news, in the papers, via social media, and unfortunately, on Christian media as well. You and I know that this peddling of fear isn't going away anytime soon. Your local news outlet is not going to start reporting on the thousands of planes that landed safely today. Fear generates viewership and is an effective clickbait for online publications.

It is vital that we do not let fear take over our hearts.

However, it is vital that we do not let fear take over our hearts. As believers, we have no business feeding on fear. If your mind is entangled with knots of anxiety, perhaps it's time for you to examine your mental diet. What have you, consciously or unconsciously, been meditating on? Are you ingesting and believing everything you see in the news reports, or are you living by what the Lord Jesus has purchased for you at Calvary?

The Place of Rest

I want to share with you a powerful key from the very first verse of Psalm 91, the prayer of protection. Read it with me (boldface mine):

> *He who **dwells** in the secret place of the Most High*
> *Shall abide under the shadow of the Almighty.*

The Hebrew word for "dwell" is *yashab*, which means to *sit down*, to remain, or to settle.[1] So the very first thing that God wants you to do to enjoy His protection is to *rest*. His protection, peace, love, and other blessings flow in your life when you are in a place of rest.

Let's camp on the word *dwell* just a little more. Let's meditate on what it means to rest or "sit down." The Bible says that we are *seated with Christ* at God's right hand (see Eph. 2:6, Heb. 1:3). The word "seated" is beautiful—it means that you are no longer standing and working.

Under the old covenant, the priest had to offer the morning sacrifice at 9 a.m., and then remain standing for six hours until after the evening sacrifice at 3 p.m. Our Lord Jesus was crucified at 9 a.m. and He hung on the cross for six hours until He died at 3 p.m., thus fulfilling the type of both the morning and evening sacrifices (see Heb. 10:11–12). Because Jesus became the final sacrifice, the work of the priest is done and he no longer has to stand. Because our Lord cried, "It is finished!" at Calvary (John 19:30), we are today *seated* in Christ (see Eph. 2:6). We can dwell in the secret place of the Most High—a place of peace, safety, and security—because the blood of our Lord Jesus has paid for every blessing of protection in Psalm 91!

We can dwell in the secret place of the Most High—
a place of peace, safety, and security—because of
the blood of Jesus.

Now, because of the completed work of our Lord Jesus, we can have free access into the presence of our *Elyon*, the Most High. We can abide under the shadow of the Almighty or *Shaddai*. These two Hebrew names of God—*Elyon* and *Shaddai*—in the first verse of Psalm 91 alone help to put our problems in perspective, don't they? In and of ourselves, our present challenges may appear insurmountable. But when we are resting in the presence of *El Elyon*—God Most High, the possessor of heaven and earth (see Gen. 14:19)—and abiding under the shadow of *El Shaddai*—God Almighty, the all-sufficient One—all of a sudden, our adversities don't seem so intimidating after all!

My prayer for you is that your perspective of God will be enlarged by the power of His living Word. Whether you are dealing with a difficult financial situation, a sleep disorder, or plagued by depressive or even suicidal thoughts, my desire is for you to discover a God who loves you, and whose strong hands of protection are over your entire life. His divine protection, as you will discover in the course of this book, isn't one-dimensional—it covers every area that concerns you.

Growing Well Despite Premature Birth

I received this precious praise report from Carina, who lives in North Carolina:

Dear Pastor Prince,

I want to share with you a testimony regarding my grandson, Caylen.

Caylen was born three months premature, weighing 1lb 7oz. He was in the hospital for almost six months and while he was there, he had three surgical procedures. We were told that his survival rate was low. Even if he did survive, he would have significant development delays due to the extreme prematurity.

At the time of his hospitalization, his mother was asked if there was a Bible verse that she wanted to be placed above her son's incubator. She gave them Psalm 91. I don't even know if my daughter had any idea of the power of putting that psalm above his incubator. I myself did not realize how powerful it was until later.

Caylen had surgery for his heart and also two more for his stomach. He did well in all his surgeries, so much so that the doctor commented, "I don't think he realizes he is supposed to be sick."

My grandson is now six years old with no developmental delays. He is advanced in almost every area, not behind in any way or having delayed development in his mind, body, or spirit. Praise the Lord!

God took little Caylen into that secret place where he was safe and received healing. I saw firsthand how the world could not harm him and he is now a walking testimony of the power and love of God.

Thank you for ministering to him and so many others.

Oh, how reading this precious praise report warms my heart! I speak our Lord's favor and wisdom over Caylen—may he grow up to be a mighty man of God and continue to be a living testimony of His great love and grace. Thank you, Carina, for writing in and sharing this testimony of God's goodness with me. There is no doubt that there is power in the Word of God. There is healing power in the prayer of protection!

There is healing power in the prayer of protection.

Is the Secret Place for a Select Few?

Carina mentioned that God took little Caylen into the "secret place." Where is this secret place and how do you get there? Before I answer this question, I want you to be careful of preaching and teaching about Psalm 91 that make "the secret place of the Most High" a place that only an elite few can go to, while the rest of us have no access to it because we haven't done enough, like pray for eight hours. Usually, the person who teaches along these lines is trying to say that there is a standard of holiness that you must attain before you can reach the secret place of the Most High. Now, if this is true and it takes eight hours of prayer at home to be in the secret place of the Most High, then how about those of us who have full-time jobs and can't pray for eight hours, and who really need protection?

Think about it for a moment. Who needs more protection—the one praying in the safety of his home or the one working out there? Clearly, it is the guy who is working out there in the world where acci-dents are possible and where he is exposed to all kinds of viruses. Yet, according to this teaching, he cannot access the secret place because he has not prayed eight hours a day! Does this even make sense to you? That's why I don't like teaching that makes certain people—especially the preacher—appear like they are part of an elite few. The Lord's blessings are not just for an elite few. If a blessing is from our Lord, *everyone* can have access to it. The young and the old, the strong and the weak, the rich and the poor—*all* have access by faith to His blessings that are freely given. Can I have a good Amen?

The Secret Place—in Christ

Let me tell you where the secret place of the Most High is. The secret place of the Most High is a place where you are *in Christ*. Wouldn't you agree that being in Christ is to be in the safest hiding place? How did you get to be in Christ? By receiving the Lord Jesus as your personal Lord and Savior. Once you are a born-again believer, our heavenly Father sees you in Christ. You are safe, protected, and secure in *the* hiding place!

The secret place of the Most High is being in Christ, *the safest hiding place.*

Remember how Noah was safe in the ark when the floodwaters came? While Noah was not perfect, God saw him as righteous because of his faith in God (see Heb. 11:7). When the flood came, everyone outside the ark died, but Noah and his family were protected and saved. Why? Because they were in the ark, which is a type of Christ, who is our salvation (see Acts 4:12).

The ark didn't have windows along its sides, only near the roof. The truth here is that God does not want you to focus on all the darkness, terror, and evil that are around you and in the world. He wants you to look up and know that His Son is coming back for you. I want you to see something else: I believe there were times when Noah might have lost his balance and fallen as the storm waters crashed against the ark. But Noah fell *in* the ark; he never fell *out* of the ark.

Similarly, for the believer today, when the devil tempts you and you fall, you don't fall out of your position in Christ, you are still *in* Christ. In the book of Proverbs, it says, "For a righteous *man* may fall seven times and rise again" (Prov. 24:16). You see, a believer doesn't fall in and out of righteousness. Our righteousness today is a gift from our Lord Jesus Christ (see Rom. 5:17). This means that even though we may fail from time to time because we are imperfect human beings, we are still in Christ our ark and do not forfeit His blessings of protection.

Now, in case you are wondering, does this make someone want to live recklessly? Certainly not! I believe that knowing you are righteous in Christ makes you live responsibly and in honor to the Lord (see Rom. 6:10–14). The revelation of our righteousness in Christ produces righteous living (see Titus 2:11–12).

Knowing you are righteous in Christ makes you live responsibly and in honor to the Lord.

Valuing the Secret Place

My dear reader, the more you grow in your revelation and valuation of how Jesus' finished work has placed you in Him—in the secret place where you are safe, protected, and secure—the more you'll find your heart at rest instead of filled with worry and fears. Something powerful happens in your heart and in your outward circumstances when you begin to value being in Christ, in the secret place of the Father's care, protection, and love.

Let me give you an illustration of what it means to value something. Suppose I brought you an old, dusty violin with two missing strings and I said to you, "Isn't this beautiful?" Your reaction would probably be, "That's not beautiful; that's old and worthless." But if I told you it's an original Stradivarius that used to belong to a world-famous violinist, all of a sudden, your appreciation of this dusty, old violin would swell and you'd ask if you could hold it. What happened? Your appreciation of the violin changed when you understood its true value.

In the same way, I want to encourage you to value the preciousness of what it means to be in Christ—being in the secret place of inseparable closeness with Him, where we have His loving presence constantly with us, watching over us, and protecting us. I strongly encourage you to keep hearing anointed preaching that keeps revealing who you are and what you have in Christ. Keep hearing grace-based teachings on God's promises to protect you, as well as praise reports of God's grace and protection over His people. Why? Because as you do, you'll begin to value being in the secret place more and more. As you do, you'll find your heart and mind more and more at rest in Him. You'll wake up every morning confident of His tender care, protection, and preservation. You'll live life full of hope and zest instead of worry and fear, and see Him deliver and protect you from whatever the enemy may throw at you!

Let's value what it means to be in Christ, where we have His loving presence constantly with us, watching over us, and protecting us.

My friend, the "secret place" speaks of a place *in Christ,* but it also speaks of intimacy, as it is a place of closeness. To be under the shadow of an object, you need to be close to that object. There are times when I travel to Israel with my pastors and the sun is scorching hot. When we are outdoors, whether it is on the Mount of Beatitudes or in Capernaum, we always look forward to being under the shadow of a tree. The difference in temperature when we are under the protective shelter of a tree is like night and day. Out in the open, we wouldn't last long under the scorching heat of the sun. But under the shadow of a tree, we can sit for hours, just discussing the Word of God. In fact, during one of our outdoor trips, we made and brought our own sandwiches and had a most refreshing time sitting and eating together under a tree.

Beloved, being under the shadow of the Almighty speaks of closeness, intimacy, and protection. It speaks of a place of refreshing, coolness, and rest. When Psalm 91 talks about dwelling in the "secret place" of the Most High, that secret place is not a geographical location, but *spiritual intimacy* with our Lord Jesus. In the same way, the prayer of protection is not an incantation or some kind of magic chant that grants you protection. It is you valuing your position in Christ and your close relationship with Him, and being found in that secret place with Him.

The secret place of the Most High is not a geographical location, but spiritual intimacy with our Lord Jesus.

He Watches Over His Own

Some years ago, I received a testimony of divine protection from a businessman who attended our church. He had been on a business trip and was staying at the Marriott Hotel in Jakarta, Indonesia. While he was in the lobby of the hotel, he suddenly heard a loud explosion. A bomb had been detonated right outside and it tore through the lobby. The blast was so powerful that he saw a body flying past him. After the dust had settled, he checked himself quickly and realized that although his shirt was splattered with blood, and debris was strewn all around him, he was completely unharmed. Amazingly, he had stepped behind a pillar at the *very* moment the bomb went off, and that pillar had shielded him from the direct impact of the explosion.

All praise and glory to our Lord Jesus who watches over His own! Just think of what could have happened if this man had not reached the pillar at the precise moment the bomb went off. Walking past it a mere second earlier or being just one second too far away from the pillar would have placed him directly in the destructive path of the explosion! With all our intelligence and smarts, only our Lord Jesus can put us at the right place at the right time and keep us in His divine protection.

Only our Lord Jesus can put us at the right place at the right time and keep us in His divine protection.

For more than a decade now, I have been teaching my church to declare Psalm 91 over themselves and their loved ones. I believe what happened to that brother in Jakarta was the power of the prayer of protection at work!

The Lord has put a *now* word in my heart for the times we are living in, and that word is "protection." I want to show you from the Bible what Jesus died to give you in the area of protection. Even as I write this book, the Lord is commissioning me to preach strongly from Psalm 91 so that you can walk in His divine protection in these last days. Psalm 91 has just sixteen verses, but is loaded with many potent promises that we can stand upon.

Hold On to His Word

Unfortunately, when we are faced with problems, whether it is a sickness, an accident, or any kind of trouble, many of us don't lay hold of and claim the Lord's deliverance found in His Word. Yet, when you do hold on to God's Word for deliverance, the devil is so afraid that the Word will become firmly rooted in your heart. That is why he will come immediately to try to steal the Word from your heart. He will point to your outward circumstances and taunt you with thoughts like, "Look, your child is still sick—where is God now? Where is the reality of Psalm 91?" At that very moment, you are presented with a choice. You can either back away from God's Word and agree with the enemy, or you can stand in faith and continue to believe His promises.

Even as the Lord put it on my heart to write this book on divine protection, He told me that there are people reading this who might think, *I have claimed the promises in Psalm 91 before and it didn't work*. My dear friend, I want to encourage you to hold on to His Word. Whatever your experience has been, the Word of God stands eternal and unshakable. If you have not experienced full protection in the past, I believe that as you hold on to His Word and persevere in faith, you will walk more and more in the Lord's total protection.

As you hold on to God's Word and persevere in faith, you will walk more and more in His total protection.

The Lord gave me this portion of Scripture to strengthen you:

> *He shall deliver you in six troubles, yes, in seven no evil shall touch you. In famine He shall redeem you from death, and in war from the power of the sword. You shall be hidden from the scourge of the tongue, and you shall not be afraid of destruction when it comes. You shall laugh at destruction and famine.... You shall know that your tent is in peace; you shall visit your dwelling and find nothing*

amiss. You shall also know that your descendants shall be
many, and your offspring like the grass of the earth. You
shall come to the grave at a full age.

—Job 5:19–22, 24–26 (boldface mine)

Let's take a closer look at the first verse: "He shall deliver you in six troubles, yes, in seven no evil shall touch you." Now, I have read this verse a number of times before, but the Lord quickened this Scripture in me, so let me share this fresh insight with you. I want to specially address those who have been greatly discouraged in the area of protection. Perhaps you have experienced a very difficult or even tragic event, or are going through a very challenging situation right now. Can I encourage you to build your faith upon His promises and not upon your experiences?

The Word of God says that in this world, we will have trouble (see John 16:33). The fact that God declares in His Word that He will deliver us from troubles tells us that we will experience troubles. But God wants us to know that the more we hear preaching on Psalm 91, the more we quote it and remind ourselves of the Lord's protection daily, the more our faith in His protection will grow.

> *The more we remind ourselves of the Lord's protection*
> *daily, the more our faith in His protection will grow.*

Faith comes from "hearing, and hearing by the word of Christ" (Rom. 10:17 NASB). The more we hear, the more we believe! The more we claim and pray the prayer of protection, the more we will walk in its blessings. That is the intention of this book—to saturate you with the hearing and hearing of the Lord's protection promises for your life until your faith is robust and overflowing. The more you believe, the more you will experience deliverance from trouble after trouble until you come to the place of "in seven," where no evil will touch you. Amen!

While we live in dangerous times, we have an almighty God who watches over us.

My dear reader, deliverance from trouble is fantastic, but there is a promise that is even greater, and that is when you are at that place where "no evil shall touch you." That's my prayer for you and your loved ones. While we live in dangerous times, we have an almighty God who watches over us. May we all increase and have a progressive revelation of the Lord's protection in these last days. While none of us, myself included, are there yet, we are on a journey of faith, of walking fully in the promises of God's protection. Let's give thanks to the Lord for His deliverance from all our troubles as we continue to believe we will come to the place where no evil will touch our loved ones and us!

2

"I WILL SAY"

I will say of the LORD, *"He is my refuge and my fortress;*
My God, in Him I will trust."
—Psalm 91:2

I will SAY of the Lord.

What are you saying of the Lord today? Are you saying He gave you the trouble you are presently in to teach you humility? Are you saying, "Sometimes the Lord heals, and sometimes He gives diseases"?

If you are saying these things about the Lord, then it's time to change what you believe about Him. If you really believe that God is the author of your problems, would you really be running to Him for help?

My friend, let's be like the psalmist who declared, "I will **say** of the Lord, '*He is* my refuge and my fortress; My God, in Him I will trust'" (boldface mine).

Your Refuge and Fortress

The Hebrew word for "refuge," *machaceh,* refers to a shelter from storms and danger.[1] This shelter is like the bunkers that many Jews have in their homes in Israel today to shelter them from small-scale attacks. In the figurative sense, when you say the

Lord is your *machaceh*, you are also declaring that He is your place of hope.

Now, look at the verse again. The Lord isn't just your refuge, but He is also your fortress. In Hebrew, the word used for "fortress" is *matsuwd*. It refers to a castle or stronghold,[2] a place of defense and protection against large-scale attacks. Isn't that a beautiful picture? Whatever you might be going through right now, you can declare that the Lord is your refuge and your fortress—your protection in both small as well as big attacks. *He* is your shelter from all danger *and* your place of hope!

---

*The Lord is your shelter from all danger and
your place of hope.*

Perhaps you have not been saying that God is behind your troubles. Perhaps you are not saying *anything* about the Lord at all. Perhaps God seems far away and you feel cut off from Him. If that is you, can I encourage you to take a break today from whatever you have on your busy to-do list, and simply take time to dwell in His sweet presence? God is not distant; sometimes we are just too distracted to hear His voice or sense His loving presence.

Take a moment and see yourself in His secret place. Abide under His shadow. Savor His favor. Receive His wisdom. And find rest for your troubled soul. The feeling of being distant from God is only a feeling, nothing more. He has promised in His Word that He will never leave you nor forsake you (see Heb. 13:5). Our Lord Jesus paid for you to have access to God's constant presence. At the cross, He cried out, "My God, My God, why have You forsaken Me?" when God turned His back on Him (Matt. 27:46). He took our place and was rejected by God when He carried our sins so that today, we can take His place of being in the constant presence of the Father and take Him as our refuge and fortress.

Are You Experiencing His Presence?

My dear reader, today you can experience God's presence in your life. Say to yourself, "The Lord is with me and I have His favor, blessings, and protection." Sense His shadow covering you. His shadow is a picture of nearness. You are not trying to get into the secret place; you are *already* there in Christ. In Christ, you can't get any closer to God. God showed Moses, the great patriarch, only His back parts (see Ex. 33:22–23). That's the old covenant—because of man's failure, God was always departing and the children of Israel only saw His back.

You can experience God's presence by saying, "The Lord is with me. I have His favor, blessings, and protection."

The picture of the new covenant is God sending His only Son, Jesus Christ. It is the picture of the father running toward the prodigal son in spite of his failures. Under the new covenant, we are seated with our heavenly Father in Christ and we see the smile on His face! That is how close you are to God today. So even if your feelings tell you that God is a million miles away, learn to trust His Word over your feelings. All you need to do is to utter the words "Father" or "Abba," and immediately you will sense that He is closer than your own breath.

In the same way, even when you don't seem to feel His presence, you can trust in Him. Trust doesn't mean that there will be no butterflies in your stomach. Trust means that even though you have the butterflies, you still act on God's Word. Whatever it is you are afraid of doing, do it afraid while keeping your trust in the Lord. There are people who are afraid to leave their house, fly on a plane, pursue a new career, start a new friendship, volunteer in a ministry, visit a care group in church, or even show up for work the next day.

Beloved, don't let fear rule your life. If you're thinking of embarking on something, most certainly, be led by the Spirit, seek wise counsel, count the cost, and make responsible decisions in your situation. Just don't allow the butterflies in your stomach to dictate your life. When you say to the Lord, "In You I trust," it doesn't mean you instantly stop feeling any fear. Trust means choosing to act on God's Word in spite of the fear.

---

*Trust means choosing to act on God's Word
in spite of the fear.*

Secrets of Protection in the Names of God

In the earlier chapter, I mentioned how we find two names of God in the first verse of Psalm 91 and how that brings comfort and strength to us when we feel afraid or weak. Each of the names of

God has a divine attribute, and understanding and believing that He is each attribute will cause that attribute to flow into our lives. The first name of God mentioned in Psalm 91 is "Most High" (*Elyon*), which means He is the Most High God and there is no one higher than Him. He is the possessor of heaven and earth (see Gen. 14:19). The verse goes on to refer to God as the "Almighty." In Hebrew, it is *Shaddai*—the God who blesses you with more than enough, more than you can contain. Man has limitations but we have a God who is abundantly unlimited.

Man has limitations but we have a God who is abundantly unlimited.

Now, the second verse of Psalm 91 contains another two names of God. Isn't this so powerful? When the psalmist declares, "I will say of the LORD," he is referring to *Yehovah* or *Yahweh*, the covenant-keeping God.[3] It is the holiest name of the Lord, and Jewish scribes treat the name with great reverence.

Do you know that Jesus' name in Hebrew, *Yeshua*, actually means *"Yahweh* saves"?[4] It is not *"Yahweh* judges." The name *Jesus* means *"Yahweh* SAVES." If you are broke, *Yahweh* saves. If you are sick, *Yahweh* saves. If you have enemies that are coming against you, *Yahweh* saves. Whatever saving you need, Jesus is the answer, for His name means *"Yahweh* saves." Hallelujah!

The psalmist in verse 2 goes on to say, "My God, in Him I will trust." Now, the word "God" here refers to *Elohim*, the God of power, the Creator.[5] The God who created the heavens and the earth (see Gen. 1:1). This is our God! He is the One we put our trust in.

Now, knowing the different names of God used by the psalmist, let's read the first two verses of Psalm 91 again (boldface mine):

> *He who dwells in the secret place of **Elyon***
> *Shall abide under the shadow of **Shaddai**.*
> *I will say of **Yahweh**, "He is my refuge and my fortress;*
> *My **Elohim**, in Him I will trust."*

In just two verses, you find four names of God mentioned. Knowing, believing, and saying He is all these to us gives us protection in our everyday situations. Before the psalm ends, God Himself says, "I will set him on high, because he has known My name" (Ps. 91:14). He will deliver and rescue the one who knows His name. Hallelujah!

Believe with Your Heart

Jennifer from Taiwan shared this powerful praise report with me:

> *I am from Taiwan but I live in Singapore, and for more than a year, I have been attending New Creation Church. When Pastor Prince started preaching strongly on Psalm 91 in 2014, I began meditating on the verses. I also began sharing the psalm with my family back home in Kaohsiung, Taiwan, and declaring it over my family members.*
>
> *On July 26 of that year, my brother, Daniel, got into a car accident and was badly injured. When my mother called and told me he was lying unconscious in the emergency room, I told her that Daniel would be fine because the Lord has promised*

to deliver us from trouble. My mother and I also took the Holy Communion on his behalf and prayed for him. Even though I was sad, I had a strong sense of peace and was not worried. In fact, I was able to sleep very well that night.

The next day in church, Pastor Prince continued to preach on Psalm 91. After the service, I received a text message saying that my brother had regained consciousness and was getting some tests done. The doctor said he was extremely "lucky" that he landed on his face. Even though he looked badly hurt, his brain and internal organs were all intact.

When my brother had completed all his surgeries and treatments, the hospital informed my mom that my brother had to give up his bed for more seriously sick people the very next day. We were very upset because he was heavily bandaged and still in pain. However, we had no choice but to comply because there were indeed a lot of people lying in the hallway waiting for help.

So my brother was brought home and my mom and sister took turns to care for him, changing his bandages and such. I told my mom then that Daniel would be fine because our heavenly Father would take care of him. We also declared Psalm 91 together.

The next day, July 31, a series of gas explosions in Kaohsiung ripped apart city streets across three districts, including the one where my mom's house is located. However, her house was untouched as the effect of the explosions and damages they caused stopped just a few blocks away.

That was truly amazing as a lot of people we know had lost their homes and were trying to escape that whole night. It was mayhem as there were multiple explosions and fireballs that *ripped up roads and overturned vehicles. People were scream-ing frantically everywhere.*

Thank God that Daniel was sent home to be cared for—my family could stay by his side and did not have to travel to the hospital and experience all the chaos out there in the streets. Also, with all the casualties from the gas explosion, it would have meant little rest and care for Daniel in the hospital, as there were simply too many patients.

My brother has experienced a supernatural healing and is recovering very well now. Interestingly, he has a red, heart-shaped wound on his leg. My brother himself says that instead of being reminded of the pain and fear from the car accident, the wound reminds him of the love, healing, and restoration of his heavenly Father every day.

We thank God for His supernatural protection and deliver-ance. He has not only delivered Daniel from the accident, but also protected my whole family from the gas explosion. A lot of things could have happened but the Lord took care of them all. We thank God that He is faithful and we thank Him for Pastor Prince's ministry.

Thank you Jennifer, for sharing with me the Lord's protection over your entire family. I am praying for your brother to experience complete restoration.

I want you to pay particular attention to the first portion of Jennifer's testimony. Look at what she shared: "When Pastor Prince started *preaching strongly* on Psalm 91 in 2014, I began *meditating* on the verses. I also began *sharing* the psalm with my family…and *declaring* it over my family members" (emphasis mine).

Can you see that Jennifer was *actively listening* to messages on Psalm 91? Let me explain what active listening means. The author of the book of Hebrews describes it this way: "For indeed the gospel was preached to us as well as to them; but the word which they heard did not profit them, not being mixed with faith in those who heard *it*" (Heb. 4:2). I pray that as you "listen" to the words in this book, you are coming alive and mixing your faith with the promises of Psalm 91. Many people heard me preach on the prayer of protection, but you can tell that Jennifer ran with the teaching, mixing it with her faith to the point that she began to share the psalm with her family members and declare the power of God's protection over them.

Believing begins on the inside. Faith begins on the inside. When the Word of God is preached, faith is the hand that takes. Faith says, "That's mine! The promises of God's protection are *mine*!" What begins inside is then reinforced outside—you begin to speak the Word out loud.

Faith is the hand that takes. Faith says, "That's mine!
The promises of God's protection are mine!"

Speak Out in Faith

But Pastor Prince, can't I just believe God's Word in *my heart? Why do I also have to say it out loud?*

Let me show you some Scriptures about faith and speaking that will help you. Romans 10:9 tells us that "if you **confess** with your

mouth the Lord Jesus and **believe** in your heart that God has raised Him from the dead, you will be saved" (boldface mine). Our Lord Jesus also said, "Whoever says to this mountain, 'Be removed and be cast into the sea,' and does not doubt in his heart, but **believes** that those things he **says** will be done, he will have whatever he **says**" (Mark 11:23, boldface mine).

Now, see what the apostle Paul wrote: "since we have the same spirit of faith, according to what is written, 'I **believed** and therefore I **spoke**,' we also **believe** and therefore **speak**" (2 Cor. 4:13, boldface mine).

Do you notice a pattern here? Faith involves *believing* in your heart as well as *speaking* with your mouth. You and I, we are made in God's image. When God first saw darkness, He didn't say, "Gosh, it's so dark." What did God do? He called forth light by speaking. He said, "Let there be light" (Gen. 1:3). In the New Testament, our Lord Jesus *spoke* to the storm and it subsided. He *spoke* to the fig tree and it withered. He *spoke* to the demons and they fled. He *spoke* to the sick and they were healed. He *spoke* to the dead and they lived.

Faith involves believing *in your heart as well as* speaking *with your mouth.*

Similarly, when we are faced with darkness in any area of our lives today, or trapped in a storm of challenges, we shouldn't be looking at the problems and despairing. We should be calling forth what we want to see! If we find ourselves caught in a dangerous situation, we should declare, "The Lord is my refuge and my fortress." If there is a sickness in our body, we can call forth our healing by saying, "Thank You, Jesus, by Your stripes I am healed!" Start speaking forth your protection, your health, and your victory today!

Start speaking forth your protection, your health,
and your victory today.

The Power of Praying and Speaking Psalm 91

Let me now encourage you with another praise report. This came from Brenda, who lives in Connecticut:

My twenty-four-year-old son, Lee, was crossing the street on a crosswalk in New York City when he was struck by a cab. He was struck on the leg and thrown onto the hood of the car before landing on the street. Miraculously, he was totally fine after the accident! He did not have a single broken bone, bruise, or even a scratch. We all urged him to go to the hospital but he refused and insisted he was completely fine.

I recall that just a few days before the accident, we were having a wonderful time celebrating Thanksgiving. Suddenly, I saw in my mind an image of Lee on a slab and dead in a morgue. I immediately dismissed that image, proclaimed that my son would live and not die, and pleaded the blood of Jesus over him.

I didn't tell anyone what I'd seen, but just thanked God for His protection for my son and all of my family members in Jesus' name. The morning of Lee's accident, I also felt led to pray God's protection over my children from car accidents— not something that I usually do.

Then, later that afternoon, I received a text from Lee telling me about the accident and that he was fine and unharmed. After hearing my son was fine, I got on my knees and cried tears of joy, thanking my wonderful Father God! I am so thankful that the Holy Spirit warned me before the accident happened so I could pray for his protection.

My son had just been awarded an awesome position in his company and we were all celebrating his wonderful new title and how God had opened up doors of favor for him. The accident happened just one day before he started his new job. As I am typing this, I just texted my son to see how he was feeling and he replied, "Mom, I am one hundred percent fine. I just went to the gym and got a monster lift in!"

I should also mention that at the time I learned about Lee's accident, I was just listening to Joseph Prince's message on Psalm 91. I used to pray it over my family all the time, but over the years, I had forgotten about this powerful psalm. I am thankful to Joseph Prince for reminding me of the power of Psalm 91. When we pray the Word of God over our children or any situation, we release His angels to work on our behalf.

Praise the Lord! We rejoice with you and your family, Brenda! Our God is such a good God, isn't He? I trust that you are beginning to see how important it is to invest your time in getting His living and powerful Word into your heart. Brenda was filling herself up with the promises of God's protection. When the Lord gave her a vision of her son being in danger, her heart was already full of faith (not fear) and she *spoke* out with authority against the evil coming against her son. When she heard about her son's accident, she was listening to preaching on Psalm 91. Coincidence? I think not. She was already building a shield of faith around her heart. Faith comes by hearing and hearing the word of Christ (see Rom. 10:17 NASB). What are you hearing today? The word of the world? The word of Wall Street? Or the word of Christ?

It is so important for you to invest time in getting God's living and powerful Word into your heart.

Build a Shield of Faith

I want to encourage you today to build a shield of faith around your family. Listen, believe, speak. Would you say it with me? Listen, believe, speak. Listen to Christ-centered messages, believe the Word of God, and speak out loud the promises you want to see in your life. I believe that the Lord wants to seal this truth in your life today. Say this out loud with me right now:

> *Lord Jesus, You are our family's refuge, our fortress,*
> *our God—in You we trust. We don't trust in our own*

wisdom, our own limited intelligence, and our own abilities. We trust in You. We trust in Your grace and Your love for us. We trust You to keep us in Your divine health and strength all the days of our lives. We trust You to keep us from terror, from fear, from dangers, from disease, and from accidents. In You we trust. Amen.

3

RIGHT PLACE, RIGHT TIME

Surely He shall deliver you from the snare of the fowler
And from the perilous pestilence.
—Psalm 91:3

Surely He *shall* deliver you from the snare of the fowler.

Not "maybe" or "sometimes," but an unqualified "surely." Not a conditional "He *might*" but a definitive "He *shall*." What blessed assurance we have that our God *will* deliver us from the snare of the fowler!

The Bible depicts the devil as a fowler. A fowler is a professional bird catcher. He lays traps and carefully conceals them so that he can ambush unsuspecting birds. The Bible also depicts the devil as a thief and murderer who comes to steal, kill, and destroy (see John 10:10).

What we need to understand is that the world we live in is a fallen world. Adam committed high treason and gave the keys of this world to the devil. Because of what Adam did, the devil is the ruler of this world. The apostle Paul calls him "the prince of the power of the air" (Eph. 2:2). That is why as long as the devil is still the ruler of this world, the world will continue to get darker and darker and there will continue to be accidents, sickness, calamities, tragedies, and deaths.

But we can rejoice in the knowledge that the devil's lease on this world is quickly running out. Apostle Paul also tells us that our Lord Jesus is coming back and all His enemies will be humbled or put under His feet, with death as the last enemy to be destroyed (see 1 Cor. 15:26).

We Are in This World but Not of This World

In the meantime, we will see the world getting darker and darker. But as believers, we do not need to live in fear. Our trust is in our Lord Jesus. We are *in* this world, but we are not *of* this world (see John 17:16). There is a very real and active fowler that is setting up snares. Even as I write this book, I'm reading and hearing reports of bombs going off, shootings, a commercial airline crashing upon landing, and viral outbreaks in different parts of the world.

In the natural, this can be extremely disheartening. But don't forget that we have a Savior who is even more real, and He has promised to deliver us from the snare of the fowler and from perilous pestilences (dangerous diseases and viruses). The bottom line is, we need to realize how much we need our Savior and His protection daily. We need to involve the Lord Jesus in our lives every day. Only *He* can deliver us and keep us safe!

We need to involve the Lord Jesus in our lives every day. Only He *can deliver us and keep us safe.*

I want to share with you another passage from Ecclesiastes 9:11–12, which also talks about the fowler's snare. Sometimes, the best way to interpret Scripture is to ask the Holy Spirit for wisdom and revelation, look for recurring themes in the Bible, and allow Scripture to interpret Scripture. What I am saying is that there is a powerful truth here waiting to be unlocked. Let's dive right in, shall we?

Ecclesiastes chapter 9 was written by King Solomon, the richest man who lived and who would ever live (see 2 Chron. 1:12). His wealth, estimated by some to be in the trillions in today's terms,[1] surpasses that of Bill Gates, Warren Buffett, and Mark Zuckerberg combined. Look at what Solomon observed in verses 11–12 (boldface mine):

> *I returned and saw under the sun that—*
> *The race is not to the swift,*
> *Nor the battle to the strong,*
> *Nor bread to the wise,*
> *Nor riches to men of understanding,*
> *Nor favor to men of skill;*
> ***But time and chance happen to them all.***
> *For man also does not know his time:*
> *Like fish taken in a cruel net,*
> ***Like birds caught in a snare,***
> *So the sons of men are snared in an evil time,*
> *When it falls suddenly upon them.*

[handwritten: all generations of human history]

We have been reading Psalm 91:1 and Ecclesiastes 9:11. Did you notice that the number 911 occurs in both passages? The number 911 is very significant for our times. It is a number that marks the largest-scale terrorist attack on American soil to date. Our hearts were broken that day, the world changed, and we will never forget what happened. While I know that chapter and verse markers in our

Bible aren't inspired, it is my personal opinion that the prayer of protection in Psalm 91 marks the times we are living in, and gives us a crystal clear reason why we *don't* have to live in fear.

Right Place, Right Time

Coming back to the above Scriptures, King Solomon tells us that the winner of the race is not necessarily always the fastest one, and the person who wins the battle isn't necessarily always the strongest. He points out that men of understanding are not the only ones who gain riches, and men of skill do not always experience favor. And then he says this: "Time and chance happen to them all."

Solomon then goes on to talk about those who are "like fish taken in a cruel net" or "birds caught in a snare." (Notice that he's saying this of the "sons of men" and not the "sons of God." As believers, we are the sons and daughters of God.) There are therefore two categories of people—those who are blessed because they find themselves at the right place at the right time, and those who are caught off guard in an evil time and find themselves at the wrong place at the wrong time. I don't know about you, but I know which category I want to fall under!

Time and Chance

Do you want to know how you can have "time and chance" happen to you like the first group of people? Then let me show you what the original Hebrew language reveals about how this can be our reality.

The Hebrew word for "time" is the word *eth*, meaning time or season.[2] The Hebrew words for "chance happen" are *pega qarah*. Together with *eth*, they present a picture not of random occurrences, but "right happenings" that are dependent on *the Lord's orchestration*. It's unfortunate that the word "chance" is used in the English translation. When you read "time and chance happen to them all," it gives the impression of random happenings, occurrences that happen as if by "luck."

Right happenings are dependent on the Lord's orchestration.

But if you study the root of the word *pega* in the Scriptures, you'll see it is from the word *paga*, which actually means to make intercession or pray.[3] Let me introduce to you at this point a principle of Bible interpretation called the law of first mention. When you are studying a word, look at the first time it appears in the Bible. There is a lot of spiritual truth and significance in the first occurrence of the word in the Bible.

Applying this principle to the word *paga*, we see in the Bible that the first time it is used is in Genesis 23:8 (NIV), where it means "intercede." The same word is also used in Isaiah 53:12 where it says the Lord "**made intercession** for the transgressors" (boldface mine).

The other Hebrew word, *qarah*, is often used in other parts of the Bible to explain God-ordained happenings. So "chance happen" should more accurately be translated as "prayed opportunities" or "prayed happenings." When you have *eth* and *pega qarah* combined here, it speaks of right-time, right-place happenings, or of being at the right place at the right time, doing the right thing as a result of prayer. I want that blessing, don't you?

Now, let's take a look at the first mention of *eth* in the Bible. This word first appears in Genesis 8:11—"Then the dove came to him in the evening, and behold, a freshly plucked olive leaf *was* in her mouth; and Noah knew that the waters had receded from the earth." The phrase "in the evening" is where you find the word *eth* (remember, it means "right timing"). What do you see? The first mention of right timing has to do with the dove—that's a picture of the Holy Spirit. It's the Holy Spirit who can guide you to be at the right place at the right time.

But look at what the dove has in its mouth—an olive leaf. When the flood during Noah's time ended, God sent a message through the dove bearing a leaf that there would be no more such worldwide flooding and destruction (see Gen. 9:15). It was a message of peace to men. What does that tell us? It tells us that the message the Holy Spirit brings is one of peace.

My friend, the Holy Spirit leads us on the wavelength of peace. Sometimes, when you are about to do something, perhaps sign an agreement, plan a vacation, or take part in some activity, you might feel a lack of peace. If that happens, please stop and take time to pray about what you are about to do, because the Holy Spirit speaks to us through the peace (or lack of it) He puts in us. He doesn't speak to us through nagging or accusations. He leads us through peace. When there is no peace in your heart, it's time for you to reevaluate your decision and listen to His leading.

When there is no peace in your heart, it's time for you to
reevaluate your decision and listen to His leading.

There's another beautiful truth hidden in the first occurrence of the word *eth*. *Eth* appears in the phrase "in the evening" not only in Genesis 8:11, but in other parts of the Bible as well (see Gen. 24:11, Josh. 10:27). I used to wonder why and when I studied it, I realized that evening time is the time of our Lord Jesus' finished work at the cross.

The Old Testament priests had two daily sacrifices, one in the morning at 9 a.m. and the other in the evening at 3 p.m. Jesus was crucified at 9 a.m. and He died at 3 p.m., thus fulfilling the type of both the morning and evening sacrifices. At the time of the evening sacrifice, all the judgment had fallen on the body of Jesus. The floods of God's judgment were ended by the sacrifice of Christ. The Holy Spirit comes to you speaking peace, telling you that there is now no enmity between you and God, because judgment has passed. You are not perfect but you can have peace with God, and you can ask Him for success in all that you do because all your sins have been judged in the body of Christ!

Pray for Right Happenings

What about the word *qarah*? The first time *qarah* is mentioned is in Genesis 24:12, when Abraham sent his servant to get a bride for his son, Isaac. The servant did not know which girl would be the right one, so he *prayed*, "O LORD God of my master Abraham, **please give**

me success this day, and show kindness to my master Abraham"
(boldface mine). The phrase "please give me success" is the word
qarah. The servant asked God to give him *qarah*—right happening.
Doesn't that remind you of what we said earlier about *pega qarah*
being "prayed happenings"? If you follow the story, you will see how
Abraham's servant was successful in his task—he found an excellent
wife for Isaac.

What I want you to focus on here is the posture of the servant. He
prayed for God's help, intervention, and leading. He had a posture
of humility. We all need the Lord in our daily lives. No matter how
intelligent we are, we can't put ourselves at the right place at the right
time a hundred percent of the time. Only the Lord can do this for us.
If we humble ourselves to hear Him, He will guide us and protect us.
The Bible says, "The humble He guides in justice, and the humble
He teaches His way" (Ps. 25:9). It is important for us to stay "low"
and lean on the Lord for wisdom, guidance, and understanding. To
pray is to adopt a posture of humility (the proud don't pray). It is
saying to God, "Father, I can't, but You can."

That is why I like to call Psalm 91 the *prayer of protection*. When
we pray this prayer, we are saying, "Lord Jesus, we can't protect ourselves, but You can. We humble ourselves before You. Be our refuge,
our fortress, and our God. Surely You shall protect us and deliver us
from harm in these dangerous times. Lead us to be at the right place
at the right time and to be with the right people."

When we pray Psalm 91, we are saying, "Lord Jesus,
we can't protect ourselves, but You can."

Another time the word *qarah* appears is in the book of Ruth, where it says, "And she **happened to come to** the part of the field *belonging* to Boaz" (Ruth 2:3, boldface mine). I like how the King James Version puts it: "and her **hap was to light on** a part of the field *belonging* unto Boaz" (boldface mine). The Hebrew word for "to come to" and "to light on" here is *qarah*. And the Hebrew word for "happened" and "hap" here is *miqreh*, which comes from the word *qarah*.[4] Incidentally, the word *happy* comes from the old English word *hap*, which is why when happenings happen the way you want them to happen, you are happy!

I don't know how many times I have heard testimonies from people who *happened* to meet an old friend and was able to minister to the friend, who turned out to be going through a personal crisis. I've also heard testimonies from people in our church who *happened* to have been delayed or who *happened* to change their original plans and, because of that, were protected from danger. My friend, none of those things happened by accident or coincidence. It was the Lord giving them *eth* and *qarah*—putting them at the right place at the right time!

I want to show you one last thing about the phrase "but time and chance happen to them all." Look at the phrase as written in Hebrew:

Pay attention to the two Hebrew characters that I highlighted—*Aleph* and *Tav* (reading from right to left). *Aleph* and *Tav* are the first and last letters of the Hebrew alphabet. They are usually left untranslated in the Hebrew, and till today, most Jewish people do not know what the two letters combined really stand for. But in the New Testament book of Revelation, our Lord Jesus said, "I am the Alpha and the Omega" (Rev. 1:8, 11). The New Testament is written in Greek, but Jesus being a Jew must have said, "I am the *Aleph* and the *Tav*." He is the first letter and the last letter. The beginning and the end. So the letters *AlephTav* point to our Lord Jesus, who has the first and final word on your situation. Your diseases don't have the last word, He does. Your problems don't have the final say, He does.

Your diseases don't have the last word, Jesus does.
Your problems don't have the final say, He does.

His signature is inscribed in Ecclesiastes 9:11 (as well as in other verses in the Bible). Do you know what this means? It means that our Lord Jesus is the One who brings the *eth* and *qarah* together in your life! When your heart is full of and dependent on our Lord Jesus, you'll end up at the right place at the right time supernaturally!

Prioritizing His Presence

A number of years ago, a lady who attends our church regularly shared that on one of her overseas trips, she got so engrossed in her quiet time with the Lord that she missed breakfast in the hotel at which she was staying. But while she was in her room, a horrific terror attack took place in the hotel's restaurant. If she had not lost track of time and had gone down to eat, she would have been at the wrong place at the wrong time. She was dwelling in the secret place of the Most High and was supernaturally led to linger in His presence that morning. She prioritized her time with the Lord over the scheduled time for her breakfast.

Now, I am not saying that you should throw out your schedule. All I am saying is, include Jesus in your schedule. You can be responsible *and* be led at the same time. But make sure it is the Spirit leading you. If you are always late for work because you are "led by the Spirit" to be doing something else, I don't have to be a prophet to tell you that you will be fired! When you are truly led by the Lord, it will lead to good success and victory.

Here's another praise report, this time from Sandy, who lives in Singapore.

Before I drive, I always make it a point to pray for protection. On March 31, I prayed as usual before I started driving toward the city. This was shortly after a big thunderstorm.

Heavy traffic had built up at a major traffic junction. I was stuck in the traffic and the cars were inching forward. Like many motorists, I got impatient and tried to squeeze ahead. But when I was just approaching the junction, the traffic light turned red. I was disappointed I had not moved as far as I had hoped to.

Then, I heard a strange sound of something cracking, and a huge old tree, which was about thirty meters tall, fell very quickly right before my eyes. It hit the roof of the car right in front of me. Because of the huge impact, the tree created a huge dent in the roof of the car and shattered the rear windscreen.

I was shocked, as it had happened right in front of me. By God's grace, the tree had fallen on a part of the car where no one was seated. I thanked God that the driver of the car emerged unscathed. Needless to say, I was very grateful to God when I realized that He had placed me at the right place and at the right time so that I wasn't hurt.

This incident further strengthened my faith in the power of Jesus' blood for divine protection over my family and me. It also gave me a stronger sense of His love for us. Even after driving for more than ten years now, I still depend on His grace and always say a short prayer before I start driving because I know that I cannot depend on my own flesh and efforts to be accident-free, safe, and healthy.

I am very thankful to Jesus for His divine protection. Without His wings of protection over me, I may not even be alive today. Thank You, Jesus. To You be the glory!

I love how Sandy doesn't take her and her family's protection for granted. Even with something as mundane as driving on the road, which many of us do every day, Sandy makes it a point to pray for the Lord's protection every time she drives. Her trust is not in her routine, nor her driving skills; her trust is in the Lord's protection.

Now, I know it's not always possible to pray the entire sixteen verses of Psalm 91. You don't have to. You can if you are able to, but you don't have to. Sometimes, before I drive, I just take a moment and give thanks to the Lord for His protection. Many times, I just pray one verse from Psalm 91. For instance, I just say, "A thousand may fall at your side, and ten thousand at your right hand; but it shall not come near you." There aren't any hard-and-fast rules. Within the prayer of protection, there are many little prayers. Each word, each line, and each verse is so potent with God's power.

Like I mentioned in chapter 1, the prayer of protection is not an incantation. It is not some magical chant that grants you protection. It is all about intimacy and relationship with the Lord. Prayer is a conversation. There is no relationship if there is no conversation. So talk to Him, commune with Him, involve Him, and listen to Him. He will lead and guide you to be at the right place at the right time with the right people.

The prayer of protection is all about intimacy and relationship with the Lord.

The snare blends seamlessly into ordinary life for the unsuspecting bird—but so does the Lord's protection and intervention when you trust Him with your protection. It may play out so naturally you may not even realize you are being protected! Before Sandy drove, she took a quick moment to look to the Lord for His protection, and the Lord allowed her to be stuck in a massive traffic jam—a very normal part of life. If not for the jam, the massive tree could have fallen on her vehicle. So even if you are stuck in a traffic jam, rejoice—it could be the Lord's way of positioning you and delivering you from some snare that you don't even know lies ahead!

4

CONSENT TO COME UNDER HIS WINGS

He shall cover you with His feathers,
And under His wings you shall take refuge;
His truth shall be your shield and buckler.
—Psalm 91:4

Do you want to know how to walk constantly in the Lord's divine protection?

It is wonderful when the Lord delivers you from the snare of the fowler. But God wants us to step into something even better, and that is the realm where we are walking in His divine protection daily. God put Psalm 91 in His Word to give us a vivid picture of what that can be like for us and to show us His heart in the area of our protection. You have seen how the Lord has marked this psalm with His signature and how four names of God appear in just the first two verses alone.

The Creator of the heavens and earth is our God and in Him we can trust!

Let's never take for granted how wonderful it is that we are safe in the secret place of *El Elyon*, the Most High God. We are under the

The ark of the covenant.

shadow of *El Shaddai*, the Almighty God. *Yahweh*, our Lord, is our refuge and fortress. *Elohim*, the Creator of the heavens and earth, is our God and in Him we can trust! My spiritual hormones are bubbling just meditating on verses 1 and 2. But you know what? Psalm 91 does not stop there. It goes on to say, "He shall cover you with His feathers, and under His wings you shall take refuge." There are so many powerful truths hidden in this simple line!

The Old Testament was written predominantly to the Jewish people, who would understand words like "His wings" and "feathers" as pointing to the ark of the covenant. Looking at the cherubim on top of the ark in the picture above, you can see why.

Of all the furniture pieces in the temple, the ark was the most holy. It was placed in the Holy of Holies, and typifies our Lord Jesus Christ. It was made of incorruptible wood and overlaid with gold. The wood represents His incorruptible and sinless humanity, while the gold speaks of His perfect divinity and deity. Our Lord Jesus was one hundred percent man and yet one hundred percent God. The lid of the ark of the covenant, where you find the cherubim, is hammered out of one solid piece of gold. It is called *kapporeth* in Hebrew and is usually translated as "mercy seat."[1] To understand the significance of the mercy seat, we have to understand the contents within the ark of the covenant.

Three items were placed inside the ark of the covenant: the stone tablets on which God had inscribed the Ten Commandments, a golden pot of manna, and Aaron's rod that had budded. The three items typify man's rebellion—man's rejection of God's holy standards, man's rejection of God's provision, and man's rejection of God's appointed leadership. God took these symbols of man's rebellion and failure, placed them in the ark of the covenant, and covered them with His mercy seat. It's a beautiful picture of His unmerited favor over our lives, of how mercy triumphs over judgment. This is the secret place where God wants you and me to live each day— not under the claws of judgment, punishment, and condemnation, but under His wings of mercy, grace, and favor. This is the place of divine protection.

Live each day not under the claws of judgment,
punishment, and condemnation, but under His wings
of mercy, grace, and favor.

No Safer Place in the Universe

Once a year, on Yom Kippur, or the Day of Atonement, the high priest would go into the Holy of Holies and sprinkle the blood of an innocent animal on the mercy seat. Let me tell you something amazing about our God. God is able to look through walls and He is able to look into our hearts. But there is one thing that our holy, powerful, and wonderful God cannot look through, and that is the blood of His Son. Once Jesus' blood has cleansed us of our sins, God does not see us in our sins anymore.

In Old Testament times, after the blood of the sacrifice was sprinkled on the mercy seat, all God saw of the ark of the covenant was the blood, and no longer the rebellion and failure of man. However, under the old covenant, the blood of the animal sacrifices only *covered* the sins of the children of Israel for one year. What happened on Yom Kippur was only a *shadow*. Our Lord Jesus is the *substance*. He is the Lamb of God who *takes away* the sins of the world, and His sacrifice on the cross was once and for all (see John 1:29, Heb. 9:12)!

In Exodus 25, the Lord told Moses,

> *"You shall make a mercy seat of pure gold; two and a half cubits* shall be *its length and a cubit and a half its width. And you shall make two cherubim of gold; of hammered work you shall make them at the two ends of the mercy seat. Make one cherub at one end, and the other cherub at the other end; you shall make the cherubim at the two ends of it* of one piece *with the mercy seat. And the cherubim shall stretch out their wings above, covering the mercy seat with their wings, and they shall face one another; the faces of the cherubim shall be toward the mercy seat. You shall put the mercy seat on top of the ark, and in the ark you shall put the Testimony that I will give you. And there I will meet with you, and I will speak with you from above the mercy seat, from between*

> *the two cherubim which are on the ark of the Testimony,*
> *about everything which I will give you in commandment*
> *to the children of Israel."*
>
> —*Exodus 25:17–22*

Where will the Lord speak from? From above the mercy seat. That is what my ministry is all about. I am preaching from above the mercy seat, preaching about His mercy and grace, about His shed blood, and about His finished work. There are people who are preaching from the judgment seat, preaching about the law and how we have fallen short. The wages of sin is death. Under the law, there is no escaping death. But this ministry is all about the Lord's mercy, grace, favor, love, and protection. Under grace, Jesus died our death on the cross. He was punished with the death we deserved for our sins. He gave up His protection on the cross, so that we may walk in divine protection today. Hallelujah!

Jesus gave up His protection on the cross, so that we may walk in divine protection today.

I want you to read this account from the Gospel of John:

> *But Mary stood outside by the tomb weeping, and as she*
> *wept she stooped down and looked into the tomb. And*
> *she saw two angels in white sitting, one at the head and*
> *the other at the feet, where the body of Jesus had lain.*
>
> —*John 20:11–12*

Do you know what Mary saw as she looked into the tomb? She saw the *substance* of the ark of the covenant. Just as there were two cherubim or angels on the mercy seat, there were two angels sitting where Jesus had lain—one at the head and the other at the feet. (For such a significant event—our Lord's resurrection—I personally believe that it was the two archangels, Michael and Gabriel.) It was an empty tomb that our Savior was laid in after He had paid the full price for our sins with His own blood. Today, this tomb remains empty because all our sins are forgiven and our Lord is risen! Our hope, confidence, and assurance of salvation are found in the nail-pierced hands of our resurrected Savior. The mercy seat is a picture of the throne of grace (see Heb. 4:16). That is where we want to be—at the throne of grace, under the protective covering of His feathers and His wings.

Where we want to be is at the throne of grace, under the protective covering of His wings.

I want to encourage you with this praise report from Veronica, who lives in New York City.

A few nights ago my husband, Casey, and I were stuck in a traffic jam for five hours. We couldn't move the car and did not know what had happened. So we put on a sermon by Pastor Joseph Prince titled The Secret Place Where You Find Protection and Long Life.

Later, we found out that a fatal accident had taken place just five seconds ahead of us before we got stuck. Five seconds. The Lord had protected us from the accident! We are so fully blessed and deeply loved by the Lord.

Today, Casey was again protected miraculously from another car accident. It appeared that a driver had had a heart attack while driving and passed out. It led to a chain collision and all the cars in front of and behind Casey got hit. And the drivers were taken to the hospital.

Despite all this, Casey's car was completely untouched. Though Casey has always been an excellent driver, he did not dare claim the credit. Everything had happened so quickly that he could not react in time. In fact, we believe that it was the Lord who protected him once again because that very morning, Casey was reading a devotional by Pastor Prince that drew Bible references from Psalm 91. It touched on verses 1 and 4: "He who dwells in the secret place of the Most High shall abide under the shadow of the Almighty.... He shall cover you with His feathers, and under His wings you shall take refuge."

Truly, there is no safer place in the universe than under the protective shelter of our Savior's wings. What blessed assurance we can have today, knowing that even if destruction rages around us, there is always refuge and comfort in the Lord, our unfailing peace, protection, and supply.

Amen! Praise the Lord! Veronica, I completely agree with you that there is no safer place in the universe than under His wings, and I rejoice with you over your amazing testimonies of the Lord's protection!

There is no safer place in the universe than under
His wings.

Gathered under His wings

There's another beautiful picture hidden in verse 4 of Psalm 91. It's a picture of a mother hen protecting her chicks. The Gospels record how the Lord Jesus looked at Jerusalem and lamented, "O Jerusalem, Jerusalem, the one who kills the prophets and stones those who are sent to her! **How often I wanted to gather your children together, as a hen *gathers* her brood under *her* wings**, but you were not willing! See! Your house is left to you desolate" (Luke 13:34–35, boldface mine). Later, Luke records how Jesus *wept* over Jerusalem, saying, "For days will come upon you when your enemies will build an embankment around you, surround you and close you in on every side, and level you, and your children within you, to the ground; and they will not leave in you one stone upon another, because you did not know the time of your visitation" (Luke 19:43–44).

The Greek word for "wept" in verse 41 is *klaio*, and it means to be so affected emotionally as to sob and wail aloud.[2] Can you see the Lord's tender mercies toward Israel as He shed much tears over her? He wished that He could gather Israel under His feathers as a mother hen gathers her chicks under her wings, but Israel rejected Him. The Lord could not force His protection on them because they were not willing to accept it. I believe that as our Lord wept, He foresaw not only the Roman siege of Jerusalem, when the temple was burned to the ground and many of the Jews killed or sold as slaves, but He also foresaw the horrors of the Holocaust.

Notice that the Lord said, "But you were not willing!" This clearly tells us that the Lord will not force on us His protection if we are not willing to come under His wings. Beloved, are you willing to have the Lord Jesus protect you and your family today? Are you willing to take Him as your refuge? Then tell Him. Let's never take our Lord's protection for granted. Instead, let's take time daily to let Him know that we are putting our trust in Him for His covering and protection.

Let's take time daily to let Him know that we are putting our trust in Him for His covering and protection.

Do you want to know what happens when you do that? Look at what Boaz said to Ruth: "The LORD repay your work, and a full reward be given you by the LORD God of Israel, under whose wings you have come for refuge" (Ruth 2:12). Wow! It was already a privilege for this Moabite outcast, who was disqualified by the law, to find refuge under the wings of the God of Israel. But God even rewarded her for doing so. In the same way, it is a privilege for us to be able to take refuge under His wings. Yet when we tell the Lord that we need Him and want His refuge, He gives us a full reward for trusting Him and for coming under His wings. What a God!

Intimacy with the Lord

The Lord does not want you to simply claim His promises of protection. He wants you to come close to Him. Running to Him and coming under His feathers speak of closeness. It's not about how many times you have recited Psalm 91; it's about having an intimate relationship with Him. As a child, if it was thundering at night and I was afraid, I would run into my parents' room, jump into their bed, and hide in my mother's arms. After a while, I would fall into a deep sleep even if the storm was still raging outside. You see, you don't have to learn the seven steps of overcoming fear. Having the presence of a loving parent right with you is enough to drive out fear. Our Lord Jesus who loves you wants you to come close to Him and to take shelter in His love. Will you do that today?

Our Lord Jesus who loves you wants you to come close to Him and take shelter in His love. Will you do that today?

I heard the story of a farmer whose farmhouse got burned down. As he walked around the smoldering wreckage, he saw the burned carcasses of his chickens. He happened to move the blackened body of one of the hens with his foot, and to his astonishment, little chicks came running out from under the body. What happened? They had taken refuge under the wings of their mother, who had given her life to save her little ones.

That's a picture of what our Lord Jesus did when He took upon His own body the full punishment for our sins. The fire of God's judgment fell, not upon the scribes and Pharisees who had rejected the Messiah, and not upon the Roman soldiers who nailed Him to the cross, but upon His own beloved Son—for the nation of Israel, for the Gentile nations, for you, for me, so that whosoever believes in Him would be saved.

But here's something I want you to see: when Jesus was offered on the cross, He absorbed the judgment of God in His own body, and, as the sacrifice, He was greater than the fires of judgment. The Offering was greater than the judgment because the Offering was not consumed. On that cross, our Lord declared, "It is finished!" *before* He gave up His Spirit. The Offering remained *after* all of God's judgment was exhausted. Hallelujah! That is why we can come boldly to His throne of grace today!

I received a praise report from Victoria who lives in California that vividly illustrates how the Lord protects us when we simply come boldly to His throne of grace and humbly consent to be protected by Him. This is what Victoria shared with me:

Sometime ago, I was replaying your on-demand Web broadcast. At the end of the message, you said you would pray for our protection. I quickly put the message on pause and called my seventeen-year-old daughter to come and receive the prayer and blessing with me.

During the prayer, you prayed that we would not die in our sleep. Though we did not have that fear, we received the prayer gladly anyway.

The next morning, when I woke up, I felt really ill, to the point I didn't think I could go to work. When I went to wake my daughter to go to school, she was also unwell, complaining of the same symptoms I was experiencing. Sensing something amiss, we both went to the ER and found out we had carbon monoxide poisoning from a faulty heater!

We know and have heard reports of how people who were exposed to carbon monoxide while asleep usually died in their sleep. We believe we were saved because of the prayer you prayed over us and our receiving it. God heard and answered. He woke us up just in time so we could be saved. We give Jesus all the glory!

Thank you, Victoria, for sharing your story. What a powerful testimony of a believer who takes every opportunity to come to the throne of grace and gladly consent to come under the Lord's wings of protection!

Shielded from Every Device of the Enemy

Coming back to Psalm 91:4, we have even more reason to rejoice. The verse ends with this proclamation: "His truth *shall be your* shield and buckler." What is the shield and buckler? A buckler refers to a small round shield used for close-contact fighting. A shield is much larger, one you can dig into the ground and hide behind when spears, arrows, or rocks are being launched at you in a bigger attack. So whether it is a small or big attack, His truth—your shield and buckler—covers you completely!

Whether it is a small or big attack, His truth—your shield and buckler—covers you completely.

In Ephesians 6:16, it tells us to, *above all*, take the shield of faith to quench *all* the fiery darts of the wicked one. Why? Because the shield of faith will cover you all around. Amen! That is why the devil is after your shield of faith—he wants to make you doubt God's Word, which is His truth. Once you take up the shield of faith, his attacks against you cannot prosper. So lift up your shield!

Once you take up the shield of faith, the devil's attacks against you cannot prosper.

My dear reader, as you listen to messages about Jesus' finished work and your faith is being built, your shield is also being built. Even if you are found in the wrong place at the wrong time, the Lord can protect you when His shield of faith surrounds you and you are placed under the shadow of His wings.

One of our church members was driving to church with his family one Sunday morning when he experienced this for himself. He was driving on the freeway and came behind a van that had a queen-size mattress tied to its roof. Suddenly, the ropes that secured the mattress to the van snapped and the mattress came hurtling toward his vehicle. He and his wife braced themselves for impact, expecting the large and heavy mattress to come crashing into their windscreen, since there was no way they could avoid it in time.

Miraculously, the mattress somehow hit the road just in front of their car, bounced to the right side, and hit another car instead. Thankfully, the driver of that car was able to brake in time and did not cause an accident. For our church member, it was as if a force field—or an invisible shield—had protected his whole family! Can you imagine what could have happened if that large mattress had crashed into the windscreen of his car, which was ferrying his wife as well as their young children in the backseat? Let's give thanks to the Lord, for He is so good and His tender mercies endure forever! Truly, *He shall cover you with His feathers, and under His wings you shall take refuge.*

5

FEARLESS LIVING

You shall not be afraid of the terror by night,
Nor of the arrow that flies by day,
Nor of the pestilence that walks in darkness,
Nor of the destruction that lays waste at noonday.
—Psalm 91:5–6

I love how Psalm 91 reminds us that we have round-the-clock protection. Whether it is at night or in the day. Whether it is in darkness or at noonday. Whether we are faced with a terror or confronted by arrows. Whether pestilences threaten or destruction looms. We do *not* have to be afraid because our God, who watches over us, neither slumbers nor sleeps (see Ps. 121:3–4)!

The reality is, the world we live in seems to be engulfed in negative news, and fear seems to be the most natural and normal response. In just the short time that I have been writing this book, I have seen several reports of senseless terrorist attacks on innocent civilians, as well as horrific accidents claiming multiple victims. I have read reports of an epidemic affecting entire communities, leading to hundreds of babies being born with deformities. It is heartrending, to say the least, and my thoughts and prayers are with the families affected by these tragedies. Seeing all this, I know that many can't help but dread that the same tragedies could befall them.

But beloved, I want you to know that in the midst of all that is happening in the world, you *can* be fearless, and this comes from knowing the Lord as the God of peace.

*In the midst of all that is happening in the world, you can
be fearless when you know the Lord as the God of peace.*

How to Live Fearlessly

Romans chapter 15 ends with the apostle Paul saying, "Now the
God of peace *be* with you all" (Rom. 15:33, boldface mine). You
might ask, *Isn't God with us all the time? Why then did Paul spe-
cifically say, "The God of peace be with you all"?* What Paul was
speaking over the people was for God to manifest Himself as the
God of peace in their lives. In other words, even though God is
always with us, we may not always experience Him as the God
of peace.

Do you know what happens when God manifests Himself as
the God of peace in your life? Romans 16:20 (boldface mine) tells
us this:

> *And the **God of peace will crush Satan** under your feet
> shortly. The **grace** of our Lord Jesus Christ be with you.
> Amen.*

Do you see what the God of peace will do in your life? He will
crush every fear, every worry, and every anxiety!

Do you see *grace* in that verse as well? Grace is the only thing
against which the devil has no defense. If you are living by your
obedience and merits, the devil has power over you because he

can always point to something that you have not done. This gives him dominion over you. If you claim God's protection and healing based on what you have done, the devil, who is a master accuser, just has to point his bony finger to one thing you have failed in, and all your faith implodes. You will disqualify yourself mentally and inwardly from receiving whatever you might be trusting the Lord for.

But if grace—the undeserved, unearned, and unmerited favor of God—is the basis of your faith, the devil has no defense. That is why we put our faith in the blood of Jesus when we talk about protection. His sinless blood was shed to pay the price for the guilty one. And because Jesus paid the price, we who are in Him have a right to walk in divine health and protection. Grace qualifies us for protection. Amen! When the devil accuses you, saying, "How dare you believe God for protection, when you are (he goes on to list your failures)," you just have to point to Jesus' blood, which has paid for all your failures. With grace as your basis, the God of peace can reign over your fears and impart to you unshakable faith for His protection!

If grace is the basis of your faith, the devil has no defense.
Grace qualifies us for protection.

Perfect Love Casts Out Fear

Something else happens when you understand His grace—you will also grow in your understanding of how perfectly loved you are by your Father in heaven. God *so* loved you and me, He sent His only begotten Son to die on the cross on our behalf, carrying all our sins upon His own body so that today, we can come boldly to His throne of grace. He did it so that today, we are not as sheep without a shepherd, but we are so deeply loved and cared for by our Abba Father. We are His children and when we call on Him, He WILL answer.

We have a God who demonstrated His love for us *while* we were still sinners—when we had nothing to offer Him but our brokenness, our shame, our sins, and our disqualifications! Oh what perfect love!

We are so deeply loved and cared for
by our Abba Father and when we call on Him,
He WILL answer.

The Word of God says, "There is **no fear** in love; but **perfect love casts out fear**, because fear involves torment. But he who fears has not been made perfect in love. We love Him because He first loved us" (1 John 4:18–19, boldface mine).

Are you fearful today? Ask yourself this question: Do you know how much God loves you? You see, you can't reason away fear. But when you have a revelation of His perfect love for you, every fear in your life will be cast out. To the extent that you understand His love for you, you will live fearlessly in dangerous times!

Jehovah Shalom

I'm sure you want the Lord to manifest Himself as the God of peace when you are fearful. So let's go deeper into what the "God of peace" means. Don't forget that Paul was Jewish, so when he said "the God of peace be with you," he was saying "*Jehovah Shalom* be with you." "Jehovah Shalom" is Hebrew for "the God of peace." Now, if you look at the first appearance of the name *Jehovah Shalom* in the Old Testament in Judges 6, you'll find a tremendous revelation right there in the story of Gideon. I can't wait to share it with you, so let's dive right in.

As we read Gideon's story, we discover that the Midianites terrorized Israel day and night. The moment the children of Israel attempted to cultivate their land, the Midianites would descend upon them like a swarm of marauding locusts and destroy their crops and pillage their livestock. The Midianites were so vicious that they would strip the land until it was completely barren and bring Israel to starvation. Fearful of their cruel enemies, the Israelites had no other option but to hide in dens and caves in the mountains.

For Gideon, the news of terror attacks against his own people was constant and never ending. Another village burned down. More sheep, goats, and cattle mercilessly taken. Another farm utterly destroyed. More people left to die of malnutrition and starvation. It is no wonder Gideon was petrified and hid himself at the bottom of an abandoned winepress to thresh the measly stalks of dry grain he had somehow managed to scavenge. He was bound by fear and overcome by all the news of terror that surrounded him.

Let's see what happened to Gideon in the midst of his fear:

*And the Angel of the Lord appeared to him, and said to
him, "The Lord is with you, you mighty man of valor!"*
—*Judges 6:12*

When you find the expression "the Angel of the Lord" in the Old
Testament, it usually refers to our Lord Jesus in His preincarnate
state. Jesus Himself appeared to Gideon when he was in the pit of
fear and called him a mighty man of valor. Isn't that amazing?

Are there moments when you feel besieged by fear? Has fear
driven you into hiding, afraid that you might be the victim of
another terrorist attack, or perhaps be exposed to some virus?
When you hear reports of terror and destruction, do you feel fearful and anxious? The truth is, regardless of how you feel, when
our Lord Jesus looks at you right now, He sees you as a *mighty
man or mighty woman of courage.*

Isn't it amazing how our Lord looks at us? It's not how we see ourselves that defines us; it is how our Lord Jesus sees us that defines us.
That's why we read His Word. We read it to discover what His Word
says about us. My friend, no matter what state you are in right now
and how messed up your life might be, no matter how many times
you have failed and even if people around you have given up on you,
the Lord Jesus sees the best in you. He sees your potential, your gift-
ing, your call, and your destiny to do great things in this life!

---

*No matter how messed up your life might be,
or how many times you have failed, the Lord Jesus
sees the best in you.*

How to Be Led by His Peace

Now, pay attention to what I'm going to say. I want you to know that when God becomes *Jehovah Shalom*, the God of peace, in your life, He doesn't just soothe your emotions. He will *lead you with His peace*. For example, you may be making some decisions at your work, for your children, or perhaps even where and when to travel for your vacation. Talk to Jesus about it. He will lead and guide you with His peace. If there is peace from the Lord, then go with that decision. If there is an absence of peace and you feel a sense of restraint, then back away from it. You will find that guidance from the Lord comes very easily when God manifests Himself as *Jehovah Shalom*. In His peace, decisions don't feel forced and full of strife. In His peace, there is a rest. His peace will guide you to be at the right place, at the right time, with the right people. Let Him supernaturally lead you.

When making a decision, talk to Jesus about it. He will lead and guide you with His peace.

I wonder how many of us are like Gideon. Look at Gideon's response after our Lord just called him a man of valor: "O my lord, if the LORD is with us, why then has all this happened to us? And where *are* all His miracles which our fathers told us about, saying, 'Did not the LORD bring us up from Egypt?' But now the LORD has forsaken us and delivered us into the hands of the Midianites" (Judg. 6:13).

Doesn't Gideon remind us of ourselves? Instead of hearing what the Lord had just called him, he began to complain. "Where is God in the midst of the terrorist attacks? Why has the Lord forsaken us? Why is the Lord delivering us into the hands of our enemies?" Astoundingly, despite hearing Gideon's tirade, the Lord simply turned to him and said, "Go in this might of yours, and you shall save Israel from the hand of the Midianites. Have I not sent you?" (Judg. 6:14).

What?

First, the Lord Jesus calls this man who is in hiding "a man of valor." Now, He calls this complaining man, who is mad at God, to go in that might of his and save Israel?

Are we missing something here? "Go in this might of yours"? Shouldn't it be, "Be gone from My presence, you stinking complainer, I must have found the wrong guy"?

I am so glad that the Lord is not like you and me. He always calls the things that are not as though they are (see Rom. 4:17). And I believe that as you receive a revelation of how the Lord is the God of peace in your life, you may be fearful and complaining now, but like Gideon, God will send you to be a testimony of His protection. He will send you to all your friends, coworkers, and loved ones who are bound by fear, and He will use you to deliver them from fear!

Do Not Be Afraid

Still fearful and unconvinced, the account in Judges 6 tells us Gideon asked for a sign to confirm that he was indeed speaking to the Lord.

Gideon then presented an offering to the Lord, and fire rose out of the rock to consume the offering. Then our Lord Jesus disappeared. Only at that moment did Gideon's lightning-fast mind perceive that he had indeed been speaking with the Lord Himself. He gasped, "Alas, O Lord God! For I have seen the Angel of the LORD face to face" (Judg. 6:22).

Gideon began to panic, because in those days, they believed that if they saw God face to face, they would die. But before Gideon could frighten himself any further, the Lord said to him, "**Peace** *be* with you; **do not fear**, you shall not die" (Judg. 6:23, boldface mine). So Gideon built an altar there to the Lord and called it "The-LORD-*Is*-Peace" (Judg. 6:24), or in Hebrew, *Jehovah Shalom*. This is the first time the name *Jehovah Shalom* appears in the Bible, and the word that goes with this name is "you shall not die."

According to the *Strong's Concordance*, the word *shalom* refers to completeness, safety, soundness, welfare, health, and supply. It also refers to peace, quiet, tranquility, and contentment, as well as friendship in human relationships and with God in a covenant relationship.[1] So if you think that *Jehovah Shalom* just gives you peace of mind, you are wrong. When you receive the Lord as *Jehovah Shalom* in your life, you are receiving so much more!

My dear friends, I believe with all my heart that the Lord wants to speak to you today about the world we live in. Like Gideon, we may be surrounded by bad news, like news of diseases such as Ebola and Zika, of bomb attacks, of random shootings, of hijackings, of missile strikes, and of fatal accidents. But God has already foreseen the problems that we will face in this day and age, and His protection and covering over us is all-encompassing.

*God has already foreseen the problems that we will face in
this day and age, and His protection and covering over us
is all-encompassing.*

When Psalm 91 says you shall not be afraid of "the pestilence that walks in darkness," it speaks of every epidemic, every virus, every deadly disease, and every outbreak. When it mentions "the destruction that lays waste at noonday," it covers all accidents and outward destruction. When it talks about the "arrow that flies by day," it covers all projectiles, including even modern missiles that can shoot down planes.

Do you know what it means for something to "walk in darkness"? Doctors might tell you that they do not know what disease is developing in your body. Now, as a child of God, you can claim His promise straightaway and say, "I will *not* be afraid of the disease that walks in darkness." Do the necessary medical checks and consult with medical professionals, but do it without fear. Do it with your *Jehovah Shalom*. When you take God as your *Jehovah Shalom*, this is what He says to you: "Do not fear, you shall not die."

Some years ago, there was an outbreak of severe acute respiratory syndrome (SARS) in my nation of Singapore. A young woman was infected while abroad and triggered a series of transmissions after she returned to Singapore. The deadly SARS virus infected 238 other people. Sadly, 33 of them died. Outside of Singapore, more than 20 other countries reported infections by the virus. It was a global epidemic, one that affected Singapore keenly. Visitor arrivals and hotel occupancy rates plunged, revenues at retail shops and restaurants took a sharp dive, taxi drivers reported fewer passengers, stock prices fell, and people lost their jobs.

Most pointedly, a report indicated that "The most immediate impact of the new disease was fear. People stayed home more and avoided public or crowded places like swimming pools and shopping centers. Many also curbed their wanderlust and shelved travel plans."[2]

A heavy cloud of fear hung over the entire nation during this time. Every day, news outlets reported new infections and fatalities. It seemed like the virus was unstoppable in its spread from place to place. It resulted in people avoiding any place where crowds gathered. But as a local church we continued to hold our services, which drew a regular attendance of over 8,000 people at that time, even within the climate of fear.

During this period, I preached strongly on the prayer of protection in Psalm 91, and the church even gave out little cards with Psalm 91 printed on them to encourage our congregation to pray this prayer every day. I preached by faith on *Jehovah Shalom* and declared that as a church, the Lord's word for us in the midst of the SARS epidemic was what He told Gideon: "Do not fear, you shall not die." By God's amazing grace, we can testify today of the goodness of the Lord that *not one person* who was attending our church regularly died from this deadly virus. Hallelujah!

Here's another praise report that I want to share with you. Tracy, who lives in Alaska, shared this powerful testimony of how the Lord delivered her brother from a serious disease that almost took his life:

> *A few months ago, my brother, Shane, contracted Guillain-Barré syndrome (a serious autoimmune disorder in which the body's*

immune system attacks the nervous system) in Laos. He was refused treatment by several hospitals in Laos and Thailand. They said he was far too advanced in the disease and that there was nothing they could do for him. He was finally able to receive treatment in a government hospital in Udon Thani, Thailand. But while there, he developed further complications and contracted three strains of pneumonia and methicillin-resistant Staphylococcus aureus (MRSA).

I flew all the way from the United States to Udon Thani in Thailand and when I saw Shane, he looked like a man hours from death, almost completely paralyzed and hooked only to a ventilator. He could only move his lips and head a bit.

I quickly pronounced God's protection and provision, and called upon the grace and mercy of God to deliver us. Within twenty-eight hours of my arrival, Shane was transported via aircraft to a private hospital in Bangkok, Thailand. He was admitted directly to the intensive care unit (ICU) where, after the first day, he was able to move his arms.

His condition improved so quickly that all the doctors and hospital staff were in shock and awe. I told them that the miracle was from God. Even my sister-in-law, who was a non-believer, saw what God was doing and wanted to know this Jesus. In fact, she gave her heart to the Lord in the hospital! She had learned so much about the love of God during that time that even her family members began asking, "Who is this Jesus?"

On the sixth day after his admission, Shane was moved from the ICU to a private room and his condition continued to improve. It wasn't easy as he had severe pain and sleepless nights, but God was there every step of the way. Throughout the day, I would lay hands on him and pray over his body. Folks back home in the United States were also praying continually.

This was war—a battle like I'd never imagined. I rarely left the hospital room and I prayed continually. Every morning, Shane and I would talk about the Lord and what He was teaching us. I also read Shane bits of Joseph Prince's book Unmerited Favor, and encouraged myself in the Lord through the Word and through Joseph's book.

Joseph's book was a source of strength. Prior to Shane's illness, I had been devouring Joseph's daily broadcasts and literature. I learned so much during that season and it prepared me for this battle. Through the healing process of my brother, I learned to lean on God and to know that He is good and always delivers. Healing is always available to us—sometimes instant, sometimes a process, but always available through the broken body and blood of Jesus.

Even though the typical recuperation time for this syndrome is between six months and three years, Shane was already walking one month later. Four months after, he was able to drive and to lift nearly 300 pounds of weight. Six months later, he went back to work full-time and was also completely delivered from depression, something he had been dealing with for a long time.

Thank you for staying true to the message of grace. It's all about Jesus and His COMPLETED work on the cross. Hallelujah! Please know that you are making a difference in the lives of so many and we are just a few among the millions who have been touched by your message of grace and truth. To God be all the glory!

Praise the Lord! Truly, we do not have to be afraid of diseases that even doctors do not know how to deal with, or as Psalm 91 describes, "the pestilence that walks in darkness." The disease was "too advanced" for Shane's doctors, but it was not too advanced for the Lord who delivered him!

Beloved, in the natural, there are so many reasons for us to be afraid. We can be fearful of terrorist attacks. We can be worried about contracting diseases and plagues. We can be anxious about destruction and accidents. Round the clock, there seems to be legitimate reasons for us to be filled with dread. But there is a realm that is higher than what we see in the natural, and I declare to you today that YOU SHALL NOT BE AFRAID. Fear is a spiritual condition, and cannot be combated with a natural answer, or by us trying to reason it away. The Bible tells us that the natural mind cannot understand things that are spiritual (see 1 Cor. 2:14). So how can you not be afraid? Invite the God of peace to reign in your life. As you do that, the robust peace of God, which surpasses all understanding, *will* guard your heart and mind through Christ Jesus (see Phil. 4:7).

When you invite the God of peace to reign in your life, the
robust peace of God, which surpasses all understanding,
will guard your heart and mind through Christ Jesus.

Beloved, as you allow the Lord Jesus to be your refuge and your hiding place, you can receive the peace that He gives. Today, hear your Lord Jesus whispering to you, "Peace I leave with you, My peace I give to you; not as the world gives do I give to you. Let not your heart be troubled, neither let it be afraid" (John 14:27). Receive

His supernatural peace, which is beyond what is logical, beyond what your limited mind can comprehend. Receive His supernatural peace that will guard your heart and become a bulwark for your mind. And may *Jehovah Shalom* fill your heart and set you free to live fearlessly in these dangerous times!

6

IT SHALL NOT COME NEAR YOU

A thousand may fall at your side,
And ten thousand at your right hand;
But it shall not come near you.
Only with your eyes shall you look,
And see the reward of the wicked.
—Psalm 91:7–8

Imagine you are in a battlefield and all around you soldiers are being slain. On one side, you see a thousand fall. On the other, ten thousand crumple one by one to the ground. You hear screams as bullets find their targets.

It is a disturbing picture and I thank God that the majority of us have not had to experience the horrors of being in a physical combat zone. But that does not mean that we are not under attack nor does it mean that we do not see death claiming its victims all around us.

We are assaulted daily from all directions by tragic newsflashes, by doctors' reports, and by attacks of the devil launched at us. And every day, we see casualties around us as we read about people dying in accidents, in attacks, or of diseases. Please understand that I am not in any way suggesting that such occurrences are equivalent to the experiences of those who have borne the brunt of armed conflicts or those who may have been in wars. What I do want to establish is that believers are in a spiritual war, and we should not be ignorant of the enemy's tactics.

When the enemy attacks you, do you recognize his weapons? The projectiles he shoots may not come with arrowheads or be filled with gunpowder, but they are no less deadly. His weapons come in the form of crippling thoughts and crushing fears. When you hear about a plane crash and are paralyzed by the thought that your next plane ride might be your last, you have been shot. When you read about a shooting at a concert venue and fear going near one in case the same thing happens to you, a "bullet" has been lodged in your mind.

In this chapter, I want to teach and equip you to combat these oppressive thoughts. Unfortunately, many believers who may experience these dark thoughts allow them to take root and grow. They water them with worry, fertilize them with anxiety, and allow them to sun for hours in their mind. How? By replaying the bad thoughts over and over again and letting them go on and on like a broken record. As a result, these believers can't sleep, they suffer from chronic panic attacks, and they might even develop autoimmune and psychosomatic conditions. What begins in the mind can take root in your heart, and can even lead to adverse effects on your physical body. When those negative thoughts come your way, you must *not* give them time to take root!

When negative thoughts come your way, don't give them time to take root.

It Is Written

It is true that you can't stop birds from flying over your head, but you can surely stop them from building a nest on your head. We can't stop the enemy from attacking our minds, but we can surely defend ourselves with the sword of the Spirit, which is the Word of God (see Eph. 6:17). God's Word is infallible, unshakable, and ever-lasting (see Isa. 40:8, 1 Pet. 1:25). Our Lord Jesus Himself showed us what to do when we are under attack by the devil. Three times He was tempted by Satan in the wilderness. Each time, His response was the same—He quoted the *written* Word of God. Against each attack, His response was to say, "It is written" (see Matt. 4:1–11).

We can't stop the enemy from attacking our minds, but we can surely defend ourselves with the sword of the Spirit, which is the Word of God.

I know of believers who say, "God spoke to me and told me that He will do that for me." I want to encourage you not to go by what you think the Lord said to you. You cannot fight the devil by saying, "God spoke to me," apart from the written Word. Please understand that I am not at all against God speaking to you, but coming against the enemy and his attacks with "God spoke to me" is not what our Lord Jesus did.

My friend, if you want to combat the enemy's attacks, stick to the pattern that our Lord Jesus showed us. In the first temptation, the devil challenged our Lord Jesus to prove His identity, saying, "If You are the Son of God, command that these stones become bread" (Matt. 4:3). Don't you think it is interesting that our Lord did not rely on what His Father had audibly spoken over Him at the River Jordan? A voice had come from heaven, saying, "This is My beloved Son, in whom I am well pleased" (Matt. 3:17). Yet, the Lord did not point Satan to the spoken word of God. Over and over again, He declared, "It is written." Now, if the Son of God used "it is written" to defeat the devil, how much more you and I need to. When fear grips your heart or evil thoughts plague your mind, *quote His written Word*!

When fear grips your heart or evil thoughts plague your mind, quote His written Word*!*

Applying the Written Word

Let me show you examples of how you can use the written Word to come against the attacks of the enemy. Let's say that while driving to work one morning, you hear some professor saying over the radio, "One in every five women will develop this disease by the age of forty." That's the time you must say, "It is written—'Surely He shall deliver you from the snare of the fowler *and* from the perilous pestilence'" (Ps. 91:3). If you do this, you are putting up a shield of faith and you are releasing power as you declare that regardless of what the reports of the world say, *your* God *shall* deliver you from every deadly disease!

Here's another example of when and how you can quote the written Word. Suppose for some reason, you are crippled by vivid images in your mind of yourself dying young and leaving your spouse and little ones to fend for themselves. Again, this is the time to speak the Word of God against those fears. Declare, "It is written—'With long life I will satisfy him, and show him My salvation'" (Ps. 91:16).

Maybe you know of an acquaintance who was killed in a fatal accident. Now, you are fearful that the same thing might happen to you. My friend, the enemy has just shot you with a fiery dart. We do not know what the other person believed. We can only be responsible for our own beliefs and lives. Perhaps your relatives or family members have died from the same illness and the enemy is now attacking you with thoughts that you will also develop diabetes like your father and uncle did, or die from the same heart condition they had.

You are putting up a shield of faith and releasing power as you declare that your God shall deliver you from every deadly disease.

My friend, if you have been entertaining thoughts like these, NOW is the time to rise up and make this declaration: A thousand may fall at my side and ten thousand at my right hand, but it shall NOT come near me (see Ps. 91:7)! For something to happen *at your right hand* means that it has to be really close to you. This means that even if something unfortunate happens to someone close to you, do not allow fear to hold you in its paralyzing grip. Speak forth the written Word of God!

Speak the Word

Beloved, it is not enough for you to merely *know* the Word in your heart. You must *say* it. That's when latent power becomes actual power. When our Lord Jesus was tempted in the wilderness, He did not merely think about Scripture. He spoke it out loud. You can memorize thousands of Scriptures, but if you don't learn to say, "It is written," and release the Word, there will be no power. God's power is there, but it is all lying dormant inside you. The moment you speak it out, it is as if God is speaking. God's Word in *your* mouth is like God speaking. Amen!

It is not enough for you to merely know the Word in your heart. You must say it.

Fear is not something you can reason or analyze away. Fear is irrational. There are some fears that come into your life and you can think to yourself, *Come on, what are the chances of that happening?* or *It's so silly to fear this.* But have you noticed that those fears still hang around? We are in a war, my friend, and the only way to defeat fear is to speak the Word of God to whatever fear you have by saying, "It is written."

It is written—"For God has not given us a spirit of fear, but of power and of love and of a sound mind" (2 Tim. 1:7).

I want you to memorize that. It's a powerful verse of Scripture.

Now, I want you to say this out loud with me: It is written— "For God has not given us a spirit of fear, but of power and of love and of a sound mind." Do you feel the power that comes with saying this aloud?

This is the truth: God has not given us a spirit of fear, but of *power* and of *love* and of *a sound mind*. I don't care what kind of fears you are battling with—fear of growing old, fear of contracting this or that disease, fear of losing your job, fear of failure. Whatever the fear that has come against you, declare, "It is written."

Whenever fear comes back, speak the Word of God.

What if the fear comes back? Then say it again! Sometimes, I speak Scriptures over my situation in the morning, in the afternoon, and in the evening. Whenever the fear comes back, I speak the Word of God. If the devil wants a fight, give him one! Give him the sword of the Spirit and he will get the *point* every time. There are many Scriptures you can memorize. Write down the Scriptures that cover the areas of your need, and arm yourself with them!

Release God's Power into Your Situation

Let me share with you how Megan, a precious lady from Minnesota, did exactly this and saw the power of God released in her situation. I'll let her tell you her story:

> I was diagnosed with throat and neck cancer. After a series of treatments, I recovered and tests showed that there was no more cancer. However, two years later, the doctors found a mass in my throat again.

At that time, I'd begun watching Joseph Prince on television. He shared a testimony of a woman who had taken hold of 1 John 4:17—"as He is, so are we in this world"—for herself and ended up not needing to have any surgery.

So I took hold of this Scripture for myself as well. My first thought after hearing the doctor's diagnosis was, "As Jesus is, so am I in this world. Since He does not have cancer, then neither do I."

Fear tried to enter my thoughts over the next several days, but I believed and kept declaring 1 John 4:17 as I was being told that I might have cancer again. I was advised to have a biopsy done and was also told that a bilateral tonsillectomy, a procedure to remove the tonsils, would be needed.

As I was being prepped for surgery, I was asked if there was anything I wanted to say. I said, "Yes. When the doctor comes in to do the surgery, she will say that the surgery is not needed and there is no cancer."

And that was exactly what happened! The tonsillectomy was canceled because the biopsy showed that I did not have cancer! When told the good news, I smiled and said, "Thank You, Jesus!"

I have your book 100 Days of Favor, *which has a page that teaches on 1 John 4:17. I keep a bookmark on that page and read it often.*

I am continually being set free by the gospel of grace. Thank you, Pastor Prince!

Praise the Lord—what an awesome testimony of the power of the written Word released through our mouths! Beloved, what the Lord did for Megan, He can and will do for you too!

The Power of the Written Word

Some years ago, I went to Israel with my pastors and we were introduced to a Jewish believer who became our guide. This man, who believes that Jesus is the Messiah, shared an incredible testimony with us. He had served as a paratrooper in the Israel Defense Forces during the fourth Arab-Israeli war in 1973. He told us how Israel had been taken by surprise when Egyptian and Syrian forces launched a coordinated attack against Israel on Yom Kippur (the Day of Atonement), the holiest day in the Jewish calendar. Israel's enemies were able to sweep in and take over large swathes of territory before Israel even realized they were under attack. This is because many of their soldiers were away from their posts, observing the Day of Atonement. Once they became aware of the attack, our guide was activated to enter enemy ground together with his platoon.

In that platoon, there were five soldiers who had made fun of him for his beliefs and who had persecuted him before the war. They told him that he had betrayed his own people and was no longer fit to be called a Jew because he had accepted Jesus Christ as Messiah. In response, he had told them that if his God were not real, they would see him die. But if Jesus were Lord, he told them, "with your eyes you will see wondrous things" happening to him right before them.

Our guide described how, during the Yom Kippur war, they had entered a forested area when, without warning, they heard general-purpose machine gun (GPMG) shots being fired all around. They were well and truly ambushed. The platoon commander in front of him was the first to get hit—he was shot in the head and dropped straight to the ground. As the second-in-command, our guide took over immediately. As he fired a volley of shots, he shouted for some of his men to shoot toward his left and called for another group of them to aim behind some rocks in another direction. But he heard no response at all from his men. When he turned to look for them, he realized that no one was there.

All his men had dived into a trench and he was the only one standing in the open. He walked over and peered into the trench. One of the men motioned for him to jump into the hole with them, screaming, "Come on, you'll die! You'll die!" Our guide did not heed their cries. Instead, he yelled, "Get out and fight. Get out here and fight!"

As he stood there, he suddenly became aware of GPMG bullets flying all around him—so many whizzing past and around him that they sounded like bees buzzing round his head. His platoon mates, including the five who had constantly teased him, stared up at him in awe. Then, he realized what was happening to him—in the midst of heavy gunfire, the Lord was protecting him. He was standing exposed in the open while they were hiding in that trench, trembling in fear. With gunfire pounding the surrounding trees, leaves started falling all around him. But not a single bullet touched him. He looked down and shouted at them, "With your eyes you see! *Now*, do you believe?"

Not a single bullet touched him. Isn't that amazing?

Our guide told us that he had grown up in a small church. On the pulpit at the front of the sanctuary was a plaque that he always looked at as a child when he got bored with the sermon he was hearing. He kept on reading those words until they entered his spirit and he believed them. Do you want to know what those words were?

> "A thousand may fall at your side,
>
> And ten thousand at your right hand;
>
> *But* it shall not come near you."

He grew up believing that regardless of who fell around him, it would never happen to him. In fact, as the bullets tore past him, he shared with us that he did not fear even for a moment that any of the bullets would hit him.

In contrast, he told us about a friend in the army who had gone to the Israeli military academy together with him. During the Yom Kippur war, his friend told him this: "I've got a feeling that I won't make it through this war. I just feel I'm going to die in this war." Although our guide told him not to say such things, his friend continued. He believed he would die in the war as much as our guide believed that he would not. Sadly, this friend was indeed killed during the war.

The enemy will always try to keep you self-occupied and in fear. God wants you Christ-occupied and in faith.

The devil is known as "the accuser of our brethren" (Rev. 12:10). He will always try to keep you self-occupied and in fear. God wants you Christ-occupied and in faith! You might have a friend of the same age who perhaps died suddenly from an illness even though he or she had seemed healthier than you. The devil will try to plant fears in your heart that you are next. By now, you know what to do. Take up your shield of faith and declare, "It is written—'A thousand may fall at your side, and ten thousand at your right hand; but it shall not come near you.'" Whatever "it" may be—cancer, disease, accidents, terrorist attacks—it shall not come near you! When you board a plane, that plane has no choice but to land safely because YOU are on board, Amen!

Meditate on Psalm 91 and allow yourself to be fortified by this prayer of protection.

Beloved, the Lord Jesus sacrificed His life on the cross so that you can stand upon His promises and claim them for *your* life. They are all fully paid for by the blood of Jesus, and the Father will see to it that you enjoy them! If you do not know what promises to claim, can I encourage you to start with the many promises listed in Psalm 91? Memorize Psalm 91 and when you are under attack, quote it the way our Lord Jesus quoted Scripture. Meditate on Psalm 91 and allow yourself to be fortified by this prayer of protection. There is such a power and authority that comes with quoting the pure and unadulterated written Word of God, and I invite you to start walking in that power and authority today!

7

DWELL SAFELY IN CHRIST, YOUR REFUGE

Because you have made the Lord, *who is my refuge,*
Even the Most High, your dwelling place,
No evil shall befall you,
Nor shall any plague come near your dwelling.
—*Psalm 91:9–10*

When I was a student, I took on a part-time job in a factory that manufactured refrigerators. Like any teenager, I had just wanted to earn some extra pocket money. It wasn't a complicated job. I was part of an assembly line and all I had to do was use an electric drill to create an opening and to fasten a condenser securely onto the back of each refrigerator. I would be buzzing away on the power drill all day, earning my keep.

At that time, I had the habit of carrying a small booklet around with me. It was my little booklet of Bible memory verses, and I would read from it and speak the Word of God three times a day. During that period, there was one particular verse in Psalm 91 that I would confess every day: "No evil shall befall you, nor shall any plague come near your dwelling" (Ps. 91:10). It was my daily confession in the morning before I left for work, and during my break times, my coworkers would see me sitting in some corner, confessing this verse. It was a very powerful revelation for me, and I really wanted His Word, and in particular this truth of God's protection, to drop into my heart.

One day, as I was assembling yet another refrigerator, I lost control of the power drill. It somehow slipped out of my hands and the drill went straight toward my stomach. Everything happened really quickly. The power drill, which was spinning at full force, hit my stomach…and it just bounced off. Some of the workers there who saw what had happened ran over, concerned for me. It was then that I realized I was completely unharmed!

The only thing that came to mind at that moment was the Scripture I had been meditating on. That day, the verse, "No evil shall befall you, nor shall any plague come near your dwelling" came alive for me. I give thanks for the Lord's divine protection over my life when I was a teenager. Don't you just love our wonderful and beautiful Savior!

The Lord Our Refuge

The prayer of protection declares, "Because **you** have made the LORD, *who is* my refuge, *even* the Most High, **your** dwelling place, no evil shall befall **you**" (boldface mine). The Word of God does not say that no evil shall befall "the world." It says that no evil shall befall *you.* The verse goes on to say, "nor shall any plague come near your dwelling," and that includes your family. Beloved, let this Scripture strengthen and anchor your heart. Because you have made the Lord your refuge, no plague will come near your dwelling. Protection from strains of viruses that science does not yet have a cure for— Ebola, Zika, or AIDS—is God's promise to you and your household!

Have you made the Lord your refuge? Psalm 118:8 says, "*It is* better to trust in the LORD than to put confidence in man." Interestingly, the Hebrew word for "trust" is *chacah*, which is the root word for "refuge" in Psalm 91.[1]

In other words, to make the Lord your refuge is to trust Him in all things. Trust Him with your plans, with your life, and with your family. Trust Him for His leading and wisdom. Confide in Him. Our Lord Jesus is not distant; He is not a Savior who is far away. He is so personal…so near you. There is safety and protection when we draw near to Him and dwell in His sweet presence, His Word, and His house.

To make the Lord your refuge is to trust Him with your life, and for His leading and wisdom.

Cities of Refuge—a Picture of Christ

There is a teaching on the cities of refuge from the Old Testament that I believe will encourage you to take the Lord as your refuge and protector and run to Him.

The Lord told Joshua that when the children of Israel entered the land of Canaan, they were to designate six cities of refuge. Back in those days, if someone unintentionally killed a person, the closest relative of the deceased had the legal right to avenge him. Sounds pretty intense, doesn't it? But that was how it was. And in His mercy, God appointed six cities and said, "Anyone who kills another person accidentally and unintentionally can run to one of these cities; they will be places of refuge from relatives seeking revenge for the person who was killed" (Josh. 20:3 NLT).

The cities of refuge were designed for people who had committed unintentional manslaughter, not for those who had carried out premeditated homicide. Deuteronomy chapter 19 explains this: "If someone kills another person unintentionally, without previous hostility, the slayer may flee to any of these cities to live in safety. For example, suppose someone goes into the forest with a neighbor to cut wood. And suppose one of them swings an ax to chop down a tree, and the ax head flies off the handle, killing the other person. In such cases, the slayer may flee to one of the cities of refuge to live in safety" (Deut. 19:4–5 NLT).

You may be wondering how all this applies to us today, and I can't wait to show you!

In the Old Testament, there are six cities of refuge mentioned, but these cities are also a beautiful picture of our Lord Jesus, hidden for us to unveil. They are shadows that point to the substance—our Lord and Savior, Jesus Christ. In the Old Testament, He is concealed. In the New Testament, He is revealed.

At the cross, our Lord Jesus put all our sins, including the sin of crucifying Him, under the category of "unintentional" when He prayed, "Father, forgive them; for they know not what they do" (Luke 23:34 KJV). He was not just referring to Israel or the Romans; all *our* sins nailed Jesus to the cross. He chose the nails and offered us complete forgiveness. Can you see how good and merciful our God is?

When you run to Him for refuge, the devil no longer has power over you.

Today, if you call upon the name of Jesus, you are qualified to run to Him and take Him as your city of refuge. Jesus is your city of refuge, and when you run to Him for refuge, the one seeking revenge (a picture of the devil) no longer has power over you. My friend, we were all sinners and the wages of sin is death (see Rom. 6:23). Before the cross, the devil had the legal right to put a death sentence over your head because of your sins. But the good news of the gospel is that Jesus took that death sentence at the cross, and in Christ we can receive His forgiveness and His protection. Hallelujah!

Uncovering Hidden Truths

I want to show you how there are no insignificant details in the Bible by uncovering hidden truths concealed in the names of the six cities of refuge. Read along with me and let's see what the Lord has for us:

> *So they appointed **Kedesh** in Galilee, in the mountains of Naphtali, **Shechem** in the mountains of Ephraim, and **Kirjath Arba** (which is Hebron) in the mountains of Judah. And on the other side of the Jordan, by Jericho eastward, they assigned **Bezer** in the wilderness on the plain, from the tribe of Reuben, **Ramoth** in Gilead, from the tribe of Gad, and **Golan** in Bashan, from the tribe of Manasseh.*
>
> —*Joshua 20:7–8 (boldface mine)*

Let me give you the meaning of the names in order of their appearance. *Kedesh* means holy place or sanctuary.[2] In the cities of refuge, people sought asylum in the sanctuaries. Then we have *Shechem*, which means shoulder.[3] Shechem, by the way, is where Jacob's well is. Our Lord Jesus met the woman at the well in Shechem. Joseph was buried in Shechem and his tomb is still there. Next, we have

Kirjath Arba, which is Hebron. *Hebron* means friendship or fellowship,[4] and is the place where Abraham and Sarah were buried. Then, on the east side of the Jordan River, we have *Bezer*, which means fortress,[5] followed by *Ramoth*, which means heights or highly exalted.[6] We end with *Golan*, which means rejoicing or joy.[7]

Now, let's put these names together to see the message for us:

> You can find sanctuary (Kedesh) on the Lord's strong shoulders (Shechem), which He offers in fellowship (Hebron). He is our fortress (Bezer) and He highly exalts (Ramoth) us above all our troubles with great rejoicing (Golan).

Hallelujah, all praise and glory to the Name above all names! The names paint a stunning picture of our Lord Jesus, stooping down to where we are, and offering His stronger shoulders to us when we are fearful and weary. What a beautiful picture of the Good Shepherd rescuing His lost sheep!

Beloved, when we have failed and are completely worn out by the fights of life, He offers His shoulders in fellowship. He is our sanctuary. He is our holy place, where we are set apart from the world. When we respond to His desire for fellowship and climb on His broad shoulders, He lifts us up.

---

*When we are worn out by the fights of life, He offers us His
shoulders and lifts us up.*

Do you remember the parable of the lost sheep Jesus told in Luke 15? When the shepherd found the lost sheep, he lifted it up and laid it upon his strong shoulders. What did the sheep do? Nothing. It just consented to be rescued by the shepherd. Jesus calls this consent on the part of the sheep "repentance"—"there will be more joy in heaven over one sinner who **repents** than over ninety-nine just persons who need no **repentance**" (Luke 15:7, boldface mine).

That is what God invites us to do today—to consent to be protected. He wants us to be on His shoulders, in the safety of Himself as our impenetrable fortress. In this place, no predator can attack His sheep. On His shoulders, you are highly exalted above all your troubles, above all danger, all attacks, and far above all principalities and powers. Yes, far above Satan, above all the powers of darkness and the snare of the fowler. On His shoulders, you are far above every sickness, disease, and every name that is named. What a great place to be!

God invites us to consent to be protected, to be on His shoulders, in the safety of Himself as our impenetrable fortress.

And does the Lord do this grudgingly? Absolutely not. The Bible tells us that the shepherd lays the sheep on his shoulders "rejoicing" (Luke 15:5). Our Lord rescues us with great joy in His heart and a big smile on His face.

The safest place you can be today is on His shoulders. Jesus is your city of refuge. In your day of trouble, run to Him! There is a wonderful verse that encapsulates this: "The beloved of the LORD shall dwell in safety by Him, *who* shelters him all the day long; and he shall dwell between His shoulders" (Deut. 33:12). When you make the Lord your refuge and dwelling place, you shall dwell safely in Him and no evil shall befall you, nor shall any plague come near your dwelling!

The Local Church as a Place of Refuge

There is another type hidden in the teaching on the cities of refuge, and that is the picture of the local church. The six cities are scattered across the land so a person can flee to the nearest one to take refuge. It is a picture of local churches scattered all around the world. The local church, my friend, is a place of refuge. The church is not man's idea; it is God's idea. It is a place where all the guilty, where all who are suffering from condemnation, and where those who are being pursued can come and take refuge. You see, it is not God's heart for you to take this journey of faith on your own. Certainly, you can learn a lot by reading books or watching sermons online, but God's heart is for you to be part of a *community* of faith.

God's heart is not for you to take this journey of faith on your own, but for you to be part of a community of faith.

In the Father's house, people experience healing, breakthroughs, protection, and other blessings. God the Father raised Jesus from the dead and seated Him at His right hand in the heavenly places, "far above all principality and power and might and dominion, and every name that is named" (Eph. 1:21). This means that Jesus is far above all sicknesses, all diseases, all terror, all snares, all cancers, all depression, and all addictions. Amen!

We all agree that our Lord is above every name, but on this earth, where does this power and dominion reside? The apostle Paul declares, "And He put all *things* under His feet, and gave Him *to be* head over all *things* to the church, which is His body, the fullness of Him who fills all in all" (Eph. 1:22–23). Where is this power today in our broken and fallen world? It is found in the church! His power, His authority, and His fullness are all found in the church—our city of refuge where we can run to and find divine protection!

Find Restoration and Protection in the Church

I was in New York City for one of the events during my Grace Revolution Tour. As I was checking out of my hotel, a couple came up to me and introduced themselves. They were on holiday together with their two kids, and they told me that they had been attending Grace Revolution Church, our church in Dallas, Texas.

They shared with me how their marriage had gone through a very challenging period, and how the church and the pastoral leadership had helped them through that difficult time. Since then, the Lord has restored their marriage and family. I requested that they write in so you can hear what being rooted in a church and hearing the Word of God did for them. This is what the precious brother shared:

> *My wife and I were coming out of a rough time in our relationship. We had decided, in the middle of summertime, that our*

relationship was worth saving, and spent the rest of the summer, as well as the fall, working on our relationship and on ourselves.

It took us some time to realize that we needed to focus more on Christ rather than on ourselves and on our problems. What ultimately saved our relationship was focusing vertically on our Lord Jesus and not horizontally on each other. We were declaring, "I am the righteousness of God in Christ Jesus," which gave us a sense of how much God loves us and wants us blessed. Knowing that we are the righteousness of God through Christ is what healed our broken marriage.

Being able to rest in all that Jesus has done, and being able to hear and meditate on the Word, has been the best thing for us. He truly is the vine and we are the branches. We now know that in every situation and circumstance, Christ is supplying our every need. He is the vine that will keep us supplied and where we need to be.

Knowing that "if it matters to me, it matters to God" was the last piece of the puzzle. We learned that there is no matter too small or too inconsequential to the Lord. Neither is there anything too big for Him to tackle for us. It seems pretty simple once you have heard the truth.

Thank God for a church that pointed them away from themselves to the Lord Jesus! This brother also shared with me another precious testimony of how the Lord had protected them from the tragic terrorist attacks that took place in Paris:

To celebrate our anniversary on November 10, I wanted to do something very special. My wife enjoys cooking and baking, and loves French cuisine. We had been talking about traveling to Europe and I thought this would be a good time for us to travel to Paris for a few days to celebrate our anniversary. I had talked to a travel agent and set up a trip leaving on the Wednesday and returning on the Sunday of that week. I had planned on spending our time around Paris with a day in the countryside.

However, I did not calendar Pastor Prince's event in Dallas, as I had forgotten that it was taking place during the same weekend. Because I was trying to keep the trip a secret, my wife didn't know to remind me either! But for some reason, I told her my plan three weeks early, which ordinarily, I would not have done. She quickly pointed out my oversight and I rescheduled the trip for springtime so that we could attend Pastor Prince's event instead. I remember how I was disappointed at that time about not getting to go on the trip.

We now know that the terrorist attack in Paris started on the afternoon of the Friday I'd planned for us to be there. We saw the entire horrific ordeal unfold on the news. Had we gone to Paris as I had originally planned, we would have been there during the attack.

Pastor Prince had been preaching on divine protection quite a bit, especially over the year before. We both felt that we had experienced God's "right place, right time" protection.

We had been hearing from Pastor Prince not to take our protection for granted, and had started sharing with our boys about how we are protected by our Father. We had begun praying with them to thank the Lord for His protection over our lives.

Ultimately, we believe it was grace, perhaps even in the form of the Grace Revolution Tour, which kept us out of harm's way.

I'm not sure how close we would have been to the horrible ter-
ror acts had we gone on the trip, but I do know that God's grace
kept us thousands of miles away. We were protected, enjoy-
ing that time with our family, singing praises to God with the
church's worship team, and learning more about grace from
Pastor Prince in Dallas!

Thank you, my dear brother, for being willing to share what the Lord has done for you and your family. I pray He will continue to bless your marriage and give both you and your wife the wisdom to bring up your kids in the ways of the Lord.

Dear reader, can you see how important it is to be planted in a local church? In this couple's case, being in a church and having the wise counsel of leaders who walked the journey with them saved their marriage. The truths that they grew to be established in also blessed them in ways that cannot be measured—they were found at the right place at the right time, kept safe, and protected by their heavenly Father.

And can you sense their joy in knowing that the Lord Jesus is their vine who supplies their every need, and to whom nothing is too big or too small for them to bring? It is written in Psalm 92 that "Those who are planted in the house of the LORD shall flourish in the courts of our God. They shall still bear fruit in old age; they shall be fresh and flourishing, to declare that the LORD is upright; *He is* my rock, and *there is* no unrighteousness in Him" (Ps. 92:13–15).

Bearing fruit in old age speaks of preservation, protection, and long life. God wants you not only to have long life, but to have quality of life and still be strong, healthy, and fruitful in your old age. And the way to have all of that is to be *planted* in the house of the

Lord. Beloved, if you are not regularly attending a local church, I want to encourage you to be planted in one. As you do so, may you, your career, your marriage, and your household flourish in every way!

God wants you to have quality of life and to be strong,
healthy, and fruitful in your old age.

A Refuge from Evil

I want to bring you back to Psalm 91:9–10. Let's read it in the King James Version:

> *Because thou hast made the LORD, which is my refuge,*
> *even the most High, thy habitation;*
> *There shall no evil befall thee, neither shall any plague*
> *come nigh thy dwelling.*

Isn't that beautiful? You can make the Lord your *habitation*. First John 4:16 says, "God is love, and he who abides in love abides in God, and God in him." The more you stay in His love, the more God Himself becomes your dwelling place. No evil shall befall you and no plague shall come near your dwelling. And as you make Him your dwelling place, He protects your dwelling. No plague shall even come near your home! In another psalm, it is written, "God *is* our refuge and strength, a very present help in trouble" (Ps. 46:1). As we make the Lord our city of refuge and allow Him to put us upon His shoulders, He becomes our "very present help" even if we encounter trouble.

As we make the Lord our city of refuge, He becomes our very present help when we encounter trouble.

Iris from Australia experienced God's protection for herself when a cyclone hit the area she lived in. Read her testimony here:

A mini cyclone that lasted only a few seconds hit our street and the surrounding area recently. As I huddled in the hallway with my husband and our cat, I declared, "Thank You, Jesus, that You are the calm in the storm!"

When the wind stopped, we went outside and saw a lot of fallen trees on the road. The trees in our street were huge and as tall as thirty meters. As a result, many cars were crushed by the trees and some houses were also damaged. My husband's work car was damaged slightly but our family car was left unscathed. And praise the Lord no one was injured!

As the damaged trees were being cut down across the road, I realized something. The path of the wind had cut through a few properties across the road and when it came near our house, it stopped completely and turned around, moving back up the road! It did not come near us and our house was completely undamaged.

Everyone in our street was so surprised that the big tree in our backyard was untouched and that we had no cleanup of

our own to do. Praise Jesus! He is the calm, peace, and pro-
tection I need!

Thank you for your ministry as it feeds and blesses me so
much. What an exciting future we have in the Lord Jesus!

Wow, praise the Lord! I love this testimony—when the Lord
Himself is your refuge and your protection, even cyclones have to
stop in their tracks when they come near you!

Living in His Love

As I said at the beginning of this book, in the natural, the world is
getting darker and darker. But don't look around you and be dis-
tressed. Don't look inside you and be depressed. Look to the Lord
Jesus and be completely at rest! As children of the Most High, we can
boldly say,

> *Father, I thank You for Psalm 91. I thank You that I*
> *am in Christ. I live in that realm where no evil—no*
> *economic calamities and upheavals—shall befall me,*
> *and no plague shall come near my dwelling. YOU are*
> *my refuge and my hiding place, and I thank You that*
> *with long life, You satisfy me. Thank You, Father, for*
> *giving up Your Son to die at Calvary so that today, I can*
> *be safe and secure in the secret place of the Most High.*
> *As Christ is, so am I in this world. As Christ is seated at*
> *Your right hand, far above every principality and every*
> *power, SO AM I!*

8

ACTIVATING
HIS ANGELS

For He shall give His angels charge over you,
To keep you in all your ways.
In their hands they shall bear you up,
Lest you dash your foot against a stone.
—Psalm 91:11–12

In the days of the prophet Elisha, the king of Syria arose to wage war against Israel. Together with his chief of staff and top military generals, he meticulously strategized their attacks. The Syrian campaign against Israel was formidable. They had the latest war machines, and their skillful warriors far outnumbered Israel's forces. There was no doubt that the Syrians would prevail.

Yet, it seemed like Israel was always one step ahead of all their tactics and maneuvers. The king of Syria would deploy his forces to ambush the Israelites, only to find the Israelites avoiding that route and taking an unanticipated detour around the Syrian troops. Morale in the Syrian camp was extremely low, with the soldiers growing restless and increasingly frustrated. It was as if Israel knew beforehand exactly where the Syrian troops would be. While he could accept the chance of this occurring once, the Syrian king was furious when it happened repeatedly. Israel seemed to know his every move, leaving him greatly disadvantaged with all his cards exposed.

There could only be one answer to this, the king thought. He was convinced that there was a traitor in their midst, leaking priceless intelligence to Israel. How else could Israel learn of the exact position of his troops and circumvent them with such consistency? Incensed by this betrayal, the king called for a high-level meeting with his top aides to flush out the mole in his camp. Livid with anger, he roared at his officers, "Which of you is the traitor? Who has been informing the king of Israel of my plans?" (2 Kings 6:11 NLT).

Fearing for their lives, one of his key lieutenants spoke up, saying, "It's not us, my lord the king. Elisha, the prophet in Israel, tells the king of Israel even the words you speak in the privacy of your bedroom!" (2 Kings 6:12 NLT). Upon hearing this, the king of Syria ordered his officers to capture this so-called prophet. When his troops reported that Elisha was in the city of Dothan, the king of Syria seized the opportunity and mobilized a great army with many chariots and horses to surround the city one night. He wasn't prepared to take any risk of the prophet escaping.

Early the next morning in Dothan, when Elisha's servant awoke and went outside, he saw troops, horses, and chariots everywhere. He and Elisha were completely surrounded by enemy forces. The servant flew into a state of panic and cried out to Elisha, "Alas, my master! What shall we do?" (2 Kings 6:15).

More with Us Than Against Us

Isn't this an exciting story? I love reading the Word. Anyone who tells you that the Bible is boring honestly hasn't read it!

Put yourself in the shoes of Elisha's servant. What would you have done and how would you have responded if you woke up and found yourself surrounded by enemies intent on killing you?

You (and I) would probably have been filled with fear too.

But here's where I want you to pay close attention, because there is a powerful truth I want you to catch.

Without faltering, Elisha calmly told his servant, "Do not fear, for those who *are* with us *are* more than those who *are* with them" (2 Kings 6:16).

I can just imagine how the servant must have felt. Everywhere he looked, he saw enemy forces menacingly poised to attack. To say they were grossly outnumbered would have been an under-statement. There were just the two of them against a whole army—an army with forces so extensive they had surrounded the whole city. There was absolutely no logic in what Elisha had just said. Had his master gone mad? Couldn't the man see? How could he say, "Those who *are* with us *are* more than those who *are* with them"?

Before the servant could work himself into an even greater panic, Elisha prayed to the Lord. It was a simple prayer. There was no fanfare, no theatrics. All Elisha said was, "LORD, I pray, open his eyes that he may see" (2 Kings 6:17). And the Lord opened the eyes of the servant.

Then he saw.

He saw that the hillside around them was filled. Filled with blin-dingly magnificent horses and chariots of fire. God's army of angels. They were all around them, flanking them on every side, ablaze with the glory of the Most High. Their beauty and majesty were beyond what the servant could imagine, and as he marveled, he realized that the Syrian forces, which had looked so formidable just moments ago, were now utterly dwarfed by the angelic army.

See with Spiritual Eyes

We have been discussing in this book how to live fearlessly in dan-gerous times. I would like to invite you to think about this: Why was the young servant fearful while Elisha was fearless? The answer is this: They saw different things. The young man saw the great Syrian army. But Elisha saw an *even greater* angelic army on chariots of fire. Elisha had *spiritual insight*, which was why he could so boldly say,

> *"Do not fear, for those who* are *with us* are *more than those who* are *with them."*
>
> —*2 Kings 6:16*

My dear reader, would you commit the above Scripture to heart?

If you are in a constant fight with fear, meditate on this Scripture and fortify your heart with this promise. Whether you find yourself besieged by debts, attacked by what doctors call a terminal illness, or constantly anxious over the safety of your children, remember this verse: "Do not fear, for those who *are* with us *are* more than those who *are* with them." The God of angelic armies is with you. No weapon formed against you shall prosper (see Isa. 54:17)!

The God of angelic armies is with you. No weapon formed against you shall prosper.

He Gives His Angels Charge over You

Notice that Psalm 91:10–11 says, "No evil shall befall you, nor shall any plague come near your dwelling; for He shall give **His angels** charge over you, to keep you in all your ways" (boldface mine). Do you see that? The way the Lord keeps us from all evil and all plagues is by deploying His angelic army. What a wonderful promise! When we choose to make Him our habitation, He charges His angels to watch over us and to surround us with His divine protection.

When we make Him our habitation, He charges
His angels to watch over us and surround us with
His protection.

What does God giving His angels "charge" over us mean? Let me illustrate it like this: If I were a general in the army and I said to a captain, "Captain, I give you charge over Private Ryan," it means that this captain must protect Private Ryan at all costs, because Private Ryan is now under his charge. Do you see? In the same way the angels surrounded Elisha and his servant and protected them, they are surrounding us and protecting us today *because God has given them charge over us to protect us*!

Now, did you know that Psalm 91:11–12 was quoted by the devil when he tried to tempt our Lord Jesus? He brought our Lord to the pinnacle of the temple and said to Him, "If You are the Son of God, throw Yourself down. For it is written: 'He shall give His angels charge over you,' and, 'In *their* hands they shall bear you up, lest you dash your foot against a stone.'" To this Jesus replied, "It is written again, 'You shall not tempt the LORD your God'" (Matt. 4:5–7).

The temptation of our Lord Jesus in the wilderness is the only instance in the Bible where the devil is recorded quoting Scripture.

But the devil had deliberately misquoted verse 11. The devil misquotes the Bible because he is the father of lies. Verse 11 actually reads (boldface mine):

> *For He shall give His angels charge over you,*
> **To keep you in all your ways.**

I asked the Lord why the devil had left out the words "to keep you in all your ways" and He directed me to Proverbs 3:6–7 (boldface mine), which says:

> **In all your ways** acknowledge Him,
> *And He shall direct your paths.*
> *Do not be wise in your own eyes;*
> *Fear the* LORD *and depart from evil.*

You see, the devil didn't want to say the words "to keep you in all your ways" because that would be tantamount to reminding believers of Proverbs 3:6–7—to acknowledge God in all our ways. So he conveniently left out that whole portion. But praise the Lord, we know that *this* is what the Lord has promised: "For He shall give His angels charge over you, **to keep you in all your ways**" (boldface mine). Our part is to simply acknowledge Him in all our ways, and He shall direct our paths, protecting us along the way!

When we acknowledge Him in all our ways, He shall
direct our paths, protecting us along the way.

Wisdom for Protection

Now, if you look carefully at the Scriptures that Satan used to try to get our Lord Jesus to throw Himself down from the pinnacle of the temple, you will find that it has nothing to do with endangering yourself to test God's protection. Psalm 91:11–12 is not encouraging you to throw yourself in harm's way. It is saying that as you go about your daily walk, as you go about the course of your daily life, the Lord will protect you. The Hebrew word for "ways" in verse 11 shows this clearly—it is the word *derek*, which means path, road, or journey.[1]

As you go about your daily path, whether going to work or heading home, there are times when the enemy may have put snares ahead of you that you are unaware of. But God will give His angels charge over you, to go ahead of you to protect you from those snares. It doesn't mean that you should go and do something foolish and harmful to yourself to test God's protection! Even as we trust the Lord for His divine protection, let's exercise wisdom as well.

God will give His angels charge over you, to go ahead of you to protect you from the enemy's snares.

You may be familiar with Mark 16:18, which says, "If they drink anything deadly, it will by no means hurt them." Now, if someone challenges you to drink poison and you willfully drink it to show that it will not hurt you, that's just being foolish. Psalm 91:11 is talking about the paths you take as part of your normal life. Drinking poison intentionally is certainly not part of your normal life. What

Mark 16:18 is saying is that should you drink something harmful without realizing it in the course of your day, the Lord will protect you from being harmed!

I have a missionary friend who told me how someone had tried to poison him while he was in the mission field. In the end, the person became a believer because he saw the missionary innocently drinking the entire glass of poison—and suffering no ill effects. From that time on, he believed in the Lord Jesus, whom he knew had protected the missionary. *That's* how Mark 16:18 applies!

Walking in Supernaturally Natural Protection

I hope you realize that God's protection does not always have to come in the form of spectacular angelic interventions. I believe that every day, His protection over us is so supernaturally natural that many of us don't even realize that we have been protected!

Some of you might have experienced this before. Perhaps you were about to cross a road after checking that all was safe. Then, as you were stepping off the curb, you felt something hold or pull you back, and right then, a car sped past you. What do you think held or pulled you back? I believe it was an angel, not necessarily spectacularly, but supernaturally protecting you!

Truths about Angels

Some of you may have the impression that angels look like little babies dressed in white togas, flying about with bows and arrows.

Psalm 103:20–21 tells us a little about what they are actually like. It says (boldface mine):

> *Bless the* Lord, *you His angels,*
> *Who **excel in strength**, who do His word,*
> ***Heeding the voice of His word.***
> *Bless the* Lord, *all* you *His hosts,*
> You *ministers of His, who do His pleasure.*

From this Psalm, we know that angels are strong—they "excel in strength." Do you know how strong angels can be? When Sennacherib, the evil king of Assyria, laid a siege around Jerusalem, Hezekiah prayed to the Lord and the Lord sent one angel to the Assyrian camp. Just one angel. In one night, do you know what happened? The Bible tells us that "the angel of the Lord went out to the Assyrian camp and killed 185,000 Assyrian soldiers" (2 Kings 19:35 NLT).

Here's something else about angels: they "do His word." They do not operate outside the boundaries of God's Word. And what does God's Word in Psalm 91:11–12 say about the Lord's instructions to His angels?

> *For He shall give His angels charge over you,*
> *To keep you in all your ways.*
> *In* their *hands they shall bear you up,*
> *Lest you dash your foot against a stone.*

The Lord has given His angels charge over us. The New Living Translation says that the Lord will "order his angels to protect you wherever you go." The Amplified version says that His angels will "**accompany** *and* **defend** *and* **preserve** you in all your ways" (bold-face mine). I don't know about you but that gives me such assurance that I am covered under His wings of refuge and protection!

The Word of God also tells us that when the archangel Lucifer fell, one-third of the angels fell with him. Do you know what that means? It means that two-thirds of the angels are still on God's side. There are more angels with God, fighting on our side, than there are on the devil's side! Hebrews 12:22 tells us of an "innumerable company of angels." There are so many angels that they cannot be numbered. We may not be able to see them, but they are all around us, ministering for us. So don't be one of those believers who are more conscious of demons than angels. Remember, *those who are with us are more than those who are with them* (see 2 Kings 6:16)!

God's angels—so many they cannot be numbered—
are all around us, ministering for us.

In the Garden of Gethsemane, when the Roman soldiers came to arrest our Lord, Peter, in his zeal, attacked the servant of the high priest and cut off his ear. Jesus said to Peter, "Put your sword back into its place....Do you suppose that I cannot appeal to My Father, and He will immediately provide Me with more than twelve legions of angels?" (Matt. 26:52–53 AMPC). My friend, Jesus *allowed* Himself to be arrested. He had more than twelve legions of angels at His disposal. According to the Amplified translation, twelve legions is more than 80,000 angels!

All He had to do was pray and those angels would have been

activated. But He did not do so that night because He had already chosen to go to the cross and to die the death that we deserved. He gave up His protection so that today, you and I can claim all the promises of His protection. And as joint heirs with Christ (see Rom. 8:17), each one of us can summon twelve legions of angels!

Jesus gave up His protection at the cross so that today, you and I can claim all the promises of His protection.

Worshiping the Lord Activates Angels

Beloved, we have a resource that is greater than any attack the devil can launch against us. Would you like to know how you can activate angels in your life?

The most important key is *worship.* As you offer your praise to the Lord, that's when angels are most active. Psalm 34:7 tells us that "The angel of the LORD encamps all around those who **fear** Him, and delivers them" (boldface mine). Our Lord Jesus defined "fear" as "worship" for us. When Satan tempted Him in the wilderness, He responded by quoting a verse in Deuteronomy that says, "You shall fear the LORD your God" (Deut. 6:13). But He changed the word "fear" to "worship" and said to the devil, "For it is written, 'You shall **worship** the LORD your God'" (Matt. 4:10, boldface mine).

Beloved, when you worship the Lord, His angels camp all around you, surrounding you to deliver you. I want to encourage you to spend time worshiping the Lord. If you are going through a difficult period in your life and are fearful, choose to worship Him. Fear fills our hearts when we are occupied with ourselves, but when we worship the Lord, we become occupied with Him, His beauty, and His goodness, and His angels surround us like a protective shield.

When we worship the Lord, we become occupied with Him, and His angels surround us like a protective shield.

Angels Heed the Voice of His Word

The next key that I want to share with you about activating God's angels is the importance of speaking or declaring the Word of God.

Psalm 103:20 tells us that angels heed "the **voice** of His word" (boldface mine).

Who gives voice to God's Word? YOU do.

Every time you quote Scriptures out loud, you are giving voice to His Word, and angels will respond. When you say, "Father, I thank You that no evil shall befall me today, nor shall any plague or disease come near my dwelling," angels harken to the voice of the Word of God being spoken. Angels cannot read your mind—so speak forth His Word!

I want to encourage you to study the Word of God and memorize a few verses. When you feel swamped by fear, learn to speak out God's Word. God's power lies dormant until you speak it forth. When you do, it becomes real and powerful in your situation and comes against whatever you might be facing.

Hebrews 1:14 says that God's angels are "all ministering spirits sent forth to minister **for** those who will inherit salvation" (boldface mine). Notice that it doesn't say "minister to" but "minister for"—those who will inherit salvation (that refers to children of God—you and me). That's an important distinction—"minister for" means that they are waiting for our instructions. We need to speak to activate them. They are waiting to respond to our words; they will not automatically look into every need that we have.

Angels harken to the voice of the Word of God being
spoken, so speak forth His Word.

You activate angels when you declare, "Surely He shall deliver you from the snare of the fowler and from the perilous pestilence." Trigger your heavenly army when you proclaim, "A thousand may fall at your side, and ten thousand at your right hand; but it shall not come near you." Our Lord Jesus Himself demonstrated the importance of speaking aloud God's Word in the wilderness when three times He said, "It is written" and quoted God's Word. I don't know about you, but I intend to speak forth God's Word!

Protected from Dangers on the Road

I received a praise report from Sophia (who lives in Georgia, US), testifying of how she experienced the Lord's protection over her and her daughter.

Thank you, Pastor Prince, for letting Jesus Christ lead you in teaching the much-needed message of grace. Today, I read your Daily Grace Inspiration titled God's Angels Are Watching Over You, *and was really encouraged.*

I recall an incident when my daughter and I were driving to Florida to embark on a cruise. While driving down the highway, we found ourselves behind a big eighteen-wheeler truck. All of a sudden, a vintage-looking car tried to get between our vehicle and the truck. I thought, "Why are you trying to get in front of me? You have the whole left side of the highway to yourself."

Right then, I heard a voice inside speak to me, asking me to be quiet. So I let the car squeeze in front of us because the driver was very adamant about getting in between my car and the eighteen-wheeler truck.

Immediately after I let the car in, one tire of the eighteen-wheeler truck blew. Surprisingly, the vintage car continued to stay in front of my car, taking the full impact of all the flying pieces of the exploded tire, and blocking and diverting them all away from us.

Once there were no more tire pieces coming from the truck, the vintage car returned to the left side of the road and drove off quickly. It then dawned on me that perhaps the driver of this car was an angel of the Lord. I was so encouraged to know that God protects us in these days and times!

Amen! When God gives His angels charge over you, they go ahead of you to guard and protect you from all sorts of danger. And yes, they may even choose to travel in vintage cars. Hebrews 13:2

says, "Be not forgetful to entertain strangers: for thereby some have entertained angels unawares" (KJV).

When God gives His angels charge over you,
they go ahead of you to guard and protect you from
all sorts of danger.

Angels Put Us at the Right Place at the Right Time

I have another testimony from a key pastor in our church. He and his wife were planning for a short vacation in Hong Kong to celebrate their wedding anniversary. They had set their eyes on a particular hotel in the city. However, no matter how hard they tried, they were unable to secure a room. Frustrated and disappointed, they had no choice but to change their plans.

Sometime later, that hotel was all over the newspapers. It turned out that in the very same week that they had originally planned to stay there, there was an outbreak of a deathly disease. Someone who was staying at the hotel had died of a highly contagious virus, triggering a lockdown. All hotel guests had to be quarantined and some were found to have contracted the virus as well.

What had initially been a disappointment for this couple turned out to be God's hand of protection upon them. Who is to say that angels weren't working overtime on their behalf to thwart their travel plans and prevent them from being at the wrong place at the wrong time? After all, Psalm 91 promises that no plague would come near their dwelling.

What may initially be a disappointment to you may turn out to be God's hand of protection upon you.

May Your Eyes Be Opened

My friend, I pray that the eyes of your understanding may be enlightened, that you may know the riches of the glory of His inheritance in the saints, and what is the exceeding greatness of His power toward us who believe (see Eph. 1:18–19). I pray that like Elisha, you will be able to see beyond that which is in the natural realm, and see the legions of angels that are poised to minister for you. The Bible tells us that "the things which are seen *are* temporary, but the things which *are* not seen are eternal" (2 Cor. 4:18).

Today, we might not physically see angels, but we know they are here with us. The Lord has promised that He will never leave us nor forsake us (see Heb. 13:5). He has promised that His goodness and mercy will follow us all the days of our lives (see Ps. 23:6). Our confidence is not in what we see but in His promises that are everlasting, and as you put your trust in the Lord, I pray that you will experience every blessing that the Lord Jesus has purchased for you on the cross of Calvary!

9

TIME TO PLAY OFFENSE

You shall tread upon the lion and the cobra,
The young lion and the serpent you shall trample underfoot.
—Psalm 91:13

Do you know that as a believer in Christ, you have authority over the enemy?

There is no question that the world is a fallen place and that the devil is the god of this world (see 2 Cor. 4:4 NASB). The apostle Peter tells us, "Be sober, be vigilant; because your adversary the devil walks about **like a roaring lion**, seeking whom he may devour" (1 Pet. 5:8, boldface mine). But get this truth into your heart today—we, as believers, are not called to cower in fear like the people of the world. The devil may be the ruler of this fallen world, but I have good news for you, my friend. God's eternal and everlasting Word proclaims that "He who is in you is greater than he who is in the world" (1 John 4:4).

In Christ, we have authority over the devil and all his cohorts. In Christ, we have authority to *tread upon the lion and the cobra*. The fowler's snares shall be foiled and the hunter shall be the hunted. Our role in this increasingly dangerous world isn't to be passive and indifferent. We're not called to be sitting ducks, waiting to be devoured by the roaring lion. We are endued with power and authority to hunt down the roaring lion!

---

*In Christ, we have authority over the devil and all
his cohorts.*

The Bible records the account of one who slew a lion, so let's
study that account to see what happened. Judges 14 tells us how
Samson was in the vineyards of Timnah when suddenly "a young
lion *came* roaring against him" (Judg. 14:5). Now, pause with me
for a second. What would you do if *you* were suddenly ambushed
by a lion?

Psychologists tell us that there are essentially three possible
responses that are instinctively triggered when a person is unex-
pectedly thrust into an extremely dangerous situation—fight,
take flight, or freeze. What do you think your response would be?
I think most of us would probably either take flight or freeze. But
look at what Samson instinctively did when he was accosted by
the lion: "the Spirit of the LORD came mightily upon him, and
he tore the lion apart as one would have torn apart a young goat,
though *he had* nothing in his hand" (Judg. 14:6). Now, *that's*
taking authority! The hunter came at Samson but found itself
the hunted!

Sometime later, when Samson went by the same path again, he
looked at the carcass of the lion he had torn apart and saw a swarm
of bees and some honey in it. So he scooped out some of the honey
with his hands and ate it. It was from this experience that Samson
came up with this riddle, "Out of the eater came something to eat,
and out of the strong came something sweet" (Judg. 14:14).

There is a beautiful picture here for all of us. Instead of being eaten by the lion, Samson obtained something to eat. And from this strong predator that had come against him, Samson received something sweet. What is the spiritual truth for us today? Out of every evil and negative thing the devil throws at you today, God will make something sweet for you. Your giants will be as bread to you. God will turn every bitter adversity into sweet honey for you!

Out of every evil and negative thing the devil throws at you today, God will make something sweet for you.

Get Ready to Play Offense

Whatever team sports you follow, whether it is basketball or football, you would know that defense is vital. Without a good defensive strategy, a team will lose. However, you and I know that defense alone doesn't win the Super Bowl. It keeps you alive in the game and keeps you in contention. But defense alone doesn't win championships.

The prayer of protection in Psalm 91 has many defensive elements. We've talked about dwelling in the secret place of the Most High, abiding under the shadow of the Almighty, and taking the Lord as our refuge and fortress. We've seen how we are covered under His wings and protected by an angelic army. Now that we've got our defensive game covered, are you ready to play some offense?

Certainly, there are times and seasons when the best thing to do is to take cover and to allow ourselves to be sheltered. The Lord is our safe house, our hiding place, and our impenetrable fortress, and I love that we get to take refuge in Him. But the prayer of protection doesn't just end there. It also declares this in verse 13 (boldface mine):

> You shall **tread upon** the lion and the cobra,
> The young lion and the serpent you shall **trample underfoot.**

That's taking an offensive position. That's going on the attack. That's taking authority!

In the Gospel of Luke, we see our Lord Jesus sending seventy disciples out against the kingdom of darkness. He sent them out two by two, as "lambs among wolves" (Luke 10:3). Have you ever *seen* a lamb overpower a wolf? Of course not. You see, this authority that we are talking about is not natural authority. Like the lamb, you and I have no power in and of ourselves. The authority that I am talking about is a supernatural authority that comes from our Lord Jesus Christ, just as the strength that enabled Samson to tear apart the young lion was a supernatural strength.

---

*As believers, we have supernatural authority that comes
from our Lord Jesus Christ.*

In all the portrayals of Samson I have seen, he is always depicted as a massive and muscular man. I personally think he could have been small and scrawny, but endued with supernatural power and might from God. Watching Samson take on the lion would have been like watching a lamb take on a ferocious wolf. Naturally speaking, the odds are stacked against the lamb. But we know that He who is in us is greater than any predator that is in the world. Amen! No wonder Samson was able to tear the lion apart with his bare hands.

My friend, I really hope you are getting this! In Christ, you are far stronger than you think you are. You may not look it or feel it, but God always uses the weak things of this world to confound the wise and mighty (see 1 Cor. 1:27). Remember, the race is not always to the swift, nor the battle to the strong. It is *the Lord* who ultimately determines who shall emerge victorious. And since the Lord is for you, who can be against you (see Rom. 8:31)!

In Christ, you are far stronger than you think you are.

Look at the exchange between the seventy disciples and the Lord Jesus when they returned. The Bible tells us that they "returned with joy, saying, 'Lord, even the demons are subject to us in Your name.' And He said to them, 'I saw Satan fall like lightning from heaven. Behold, **I give you the authority to trample on serpents and scorpions, and over all the power of the enemy, and nothing shall by any means hurt you**'" (Luke 10:17–19, boldface mine). That, my friend, is the power and authority we have as believers today!

The Enemy Is Beneath Your Feet

In chapter 5 of this book, we saw how Romans 16:20 declares that the God of peace will crush Satan. Do you recall where he will be crushed? That's right, underneath our feet! Do not put the devil on a pedestal, as if he has dominion and power over you. He is a defeated foe. His proper place is not to rule over you, but to be *beneath your feet*. The Bible is very consistent and always puts the devil underneath your feet (see Gen. 3:15, Eph. 1:22). You are not at the mercy of the enemy's attacks. Remind yourself that in Christ, you are "far above all principality and power and might and dominion" (Eph. 1:21), and every lion and serpent you shall trample underfoot!

In Christ, you are far above all principality, power, might, and dominion.

Do you want to see how you can take authority over your situation by standing on the Word of God? Join me in reading this wonderful report that Gisele from Texas shared with me:

My husband had surgery for hiatal hernia. It was a simple procedure where a piece of mesh was inserted into the affected area and he was able to return home the same day.

However, he became increasingly unwell after he got home. He was feeling very bloated, had a lot of pain, and was running a fever. He was admitted back to the hospital and we spent the next week there.

It turned out that a bowel obstruction was causing all of his problems. Another surgery was planned. Honestly, we felt very discouraged and defeated at that point. Then, I remembered learning a few weeks earlier from Joseph Prince about how Christians should take charge and command symptoms to go using the Word of God. I told my husband about it and we prayed, speaking God's Word. I also commanded the bowel obstruction to be gone in Jesus' name.

Later that night, my husband went for a series of abdominal tests. These were tests that the hospital had been conducting twice daily since his admission to benchmark his progress. The next morning, when the tests were being done again, my husband started feeling great and announced that he was going home.

The doctor was thrilled with his huge turnaround and told us that the blockage, which had been detected in all the other tests done previously, was not found in the last two tests. So my husband was discharged and we went home. Praise the Lord for His protection and healing!

All glory to our Lord Jesus Christ. I love how Gisele did not take flight or freeze when she came under attack, even though as a couple they felt discouraged when they heard the doctor's report. She quickly put into practice what she'd heard me teach about exercising our authority through using the Word. She and her husband prayed, speaking God's Word over his body, *and* she commanded the negative symptoms to go in Jesus' name, as the apostle Peter did in the book of Acts (see Acts 3:6).

That, my friend, is how we go on the offensive against the enemy today. We wield the sword of the Spirit, which is the Word of God! Our authority, our strength, and our victory are found in His Word.

Our authority, our strength, and our victory are found in His Word.

Look at how the Bible describes the armor of God:

> *Stand therefore, having girded your waist with truth, having put on the breastplate of righteousness, and having shod your feet with the preparation of the gospel of peace; above all, taking the shield of faith with which you will be able to quench all the fiery darts of the wicked one. And take the helmet of salvation, and the sword of the Spirit, which is the word of God.*
>
> —Ephesians 6:14–17

Have you noticed that the breastplate of righteousness, shield of faith, and helmet of salvation are all defensive gear used to guard and protect you? The sword of the Spirit, which is the Word of God, is the only piece of the armor that is offensive. That is why, for every round of attack the devil launched at our Lord Jesus, He fought back with the sword of the Spirit—He used the written Word of God.

When we pray the prayer of protection in Psalm 91, we are praying according to the Word of God and wielding the sword of the Spirit. So no matter what report is roaring at you, be it from doctors, bankers, or from the news media, take your place of authority and lay hold of Scriptures for your situation. Fight back with the Word of God!

When we pray Psalm 91, we are praying according to the Word of God and wielding the sword of the Spirit.

The Roaring Lion

First Peter 5:8 tells us that the devil "walks about like a roaring lion, seeking whom he may devour." Isn't it interesting that he has to *seek out* those whom he *may* devour? This means that he can't devour everyone. Don't surrender your authority to him and be found among those whom he can devour! Also, did you notice that he roams about like, or as, "a roaring lion"? I asked the Lord why the devil goes about as a roaring lion and not some other creature. He led me to Proverbs 19:12, which says, "The king's wrath *is* like **the roaring of a lion**" (boldface mine). The devil is a liar and an imposter. He goes about as a roaring lion because he is imitating the King of kings, our Lord Jesus, the real lion of Judah. He wants people to think that our King is full of wrath, anger, and rage against us. He comes at us roaring with the voice of condemnation, accusation, and shame.

We have all heard that roar before. Satan wants you to have the impression that God is angry with you, that you have failed Him, and that He is not only disappointed with you, but is also downright furious with you. Now, think about this for a moment. If you believe that about God, would you be taking refuge under the shelter of His wings? Would you be taking your rightful place of authority, power, and strength? Of course not. In fact, you will flee from God!

Believers who are under a cloud of condemnation won't pray the prayer of protection. They feel unworthy of God's promises and, in fact, are expecting punishment and judgment from God. That is exactly where the devil wants you to be. When you run away from God, you are running straight into the devil's snare. You abdicate your place of authority when you abdicate your place of intimacy with God.

You abdicate your place of authority over the enemy when you abdicate your place of intimacy with God.

Beloved, you need to know this: You are loved. God is not mad at you. In Christ, you can have the confident assurance that you are forgiven, loved, and righteous (see Eph. 1:7, Rom. 8:37, 2 Cor. 5:21). The Lord Jesus has taken all your punishment at the cross so that today, you can enjoy His undeserved, unearned, and unmerited favor. God sees you *in Christ*, who is completely spotless and without blame.

Based on our own deeds, none of us qualify for His protection. But because of what our Lord Jesus has done for us on the cross, we can all come boldly to His throne of grace (see Heb. 4:16). Because of what He has done, we qualify to dwell in the secret place with the King of kings, where the phony "roaring lion" has no power over us!

Read the whole of Proverbs 19:12. It says, "The king's wrath *is* like the roaring of a lion, but **his favor *is* like dew on the grass**" (boldface mine). God's wrath against our sins was completely satisfied at Calvary, and today we are beneficiaries of His favor. In Hebrew, the word used for "favor" is *ratsown*, which means His pleasure, delight, goodwill, and acceptance.[1]

Our place of protection was purchased with the blood of our Lord Jesus Christ. In Him, we have been made righteous, and all the blessings of the righteous, including protection, provision, and length of days, are our inheritance. That's the place we are in today. Isn't that beautiful? No wonder the Scriptures tell us, "The wicked flee when no one pursues, but the righteous are bold as a lion" (Prov. 28:1). It also tells us, "The effective, fervent prayer of a righteous man avails much" (James 5:16). A righteous man (or woman) is who you are in Christ, and when you pray the prayer of protection in Psalm 91, your prayers avail much, for God answers your prayers!

As a righteous man or woman in Christ, your prayers
avail much, for God answers your prayers.

I received a testimony of God's divine protection from Sally, who lives in South Africa. Be encouraged as you read how she prayed for protection knowing that she is righteous in Christ:

> I was driving a rented car when I heard a loud bang. Within moments, I realized that the car was on fire. I immediately switched off the engine to get out. But to my horror, I could not remove the seat belt or open the door! I was stuck.

Finally, I managed to get the door opened. By then, the flames were threatening to come inside the car and I had to close the door again. A few other motorists came screaming at me to get out because the car looked like it was about to explode. They didn't know that I was trapped by the seat belt.

I called out to Abba Father and just declared, "I am Your righteousness. You are the only One who can save me!" As those words were echoing in my ears and heart, I heard a click as the seat belt was released. I ran out of the car without taking any of my belongings. When I realized that my spare keys and documents were going to be burned, I ran back to the car to try to retrieve them.

Everyone around me was screaming for me to get away from the burning car. Then one brave motorist came to my aid with a small fire extinguisher, broke the front passenger window, and retrieved my bag. By then, the fire department had arrived and was able to stop the blaze. My car did not explode after all. I praise the Lord for delivering me safely out of this dangerous situation!

I realized that the devil has long been defeated and we don't have to fear anything anymore. Thank you, Pastor Prince, for preaching the gospel.

Praise the Lord for His deliverance and protection. Sally, thank you for sharing how the Lord responded to your prayer. Personally, I wouldn't recommend that anyone return to their burning car to collect their belongings, but I rejoice with you that despite taking this risk, you were shielded from all danger!

Is There No Suffering for the Believer?

Am I saying that there's no suffering in the body of Christ? My dear reader, none of these protection truths shared from God's Word negates the fact that we are called and given the privilege to suffer persecution for His name's sake.

The apostle Paul shares in the book of Philippians, "For to you it has been granted on behalf of Christ, not only to believe in Him, but also to suffer for His sake, having the same conflict which you saw in me and now hear *is* in me" (Phil. 1:29–30). Furthermore, Paul tells his protégé, Timothy, "Everyone who wants to live a godly life in Christ Jesus **will** suffer persecution" (2 Tim. 3:12 NLT, boldface mine). Jesus Himself said that those who follow Him will be persecuted for His name's sake (see Matt. 10:22). This persecution involves other people who come against you when you live a godly life and preach the gospel of Jesus Christ. Be clear that it doesn't involve terminal illnesses, tragic accidents, or premature death.

But Pastor Prince, what about Job? Wasn't Job a righteous man who experienced terrible suffering?

I have preached a full message on Job and it is not the focus of this book to cover the full spectrum of Job's suffering. However, as bonus content for you, you can get the full audio message at no cost here: JosephPrince.com/whataboutjob. For now, I just want you to see that what happened to Job is not something that will happen to you who are IN CHRIST today. You see, one of Job's complaints was this: "If only there were a mediator between us, someone who could bring us together" (Job 9:33 NLT). Now, read these powerful words spoken by Elihu in Job 33:23–25, which describes this mediator:

"If there is a messenger for him,
A mediator, one among a thousand,
To show man His uprightness,
Then He is gracious to him, and says,
'Deliver him from going down to the Pit;
I have found a ransom';
His flesh shall be young like a child's,
He shall return to the days of his youth."

Elihu's description of a mediator foreshadows what our Lord Jesus Christ would do and be for us. First Timothy 2:5–6 tells us, "For *there is* one God and one Mediator between God and men, *the* Man Christ Jesus, who gave Himself a ransom for all, to be testified in due time." Job experienced his sufferings because he didn't have a mediator. But today, you and I do—in the person of our Lord Jesus, who died at the cross to atone for our sins and made us righteous before God. He became our ransom (the Hebrew word for "ransom" comes from the root word *kaphar*, which means "to make an atonement"[2]).

The atoning blood of Christ has canceled all the legal
rights that the enemy had against you and your family.

Today, on account of what Christ has done and become for us, God says, "Because I have found a ransom, deliver this man (you and me) from going down to the pit." Beloved, the atoning blood of Christ has canceled all the legal rights that the enemy had against you and your family. When we receive all that His perfect sacrifice at the cross has accomplished for us, we will see Him deliver us from the pit. Today, you don't have to live afraid that you will be like Job. Unlike Job, you have a mediator—Christ Jesus. In Him you can look forward to a future full of His promises, blessings, and protection (see Ps. 23:6)!

Authority over Death

At this point, some of you may be wondering, *If as believers we have authority over the enemy, why were the apostle Paul and some of the other apostles martyred? Didn't they have the authority to crush the enemies who were after their lives?*

Firstly, let me submit to you that they *chose* to be martyred—it was not something that caught them by surprise. Let me show you some evidence of this from the Word of God.

Hebrews chapter 11 recounts the amazing heroes of faith down through the corridors of time, those "who through faith subdued kingdoms, worked righteousness, obtained promises, stopped the mouths of lions, quenched the violence of fire, escaped the edge of the sword, out of weakness were made strong, became valiant in battle, turned to flight the armies of the aliens. Women received their dead raised to life again. Others were tortured, **not accepting deliverance**" (Heb. 11:33–35, boldface mine). The phrase "not accepting deliverance" tells us that they *were offered* deliverance, but they *chose not to accept it*. This was because they chose to be with Jesus "that they might obtain a better resurrection."

Listen to how the apostle Paul spoke about his life: "For to me, living means living for Christ, and **dying is even better**. But if I live, I can do more fruitful work for Christ. So I really don't know which is better. I'm torn between two desires: I long to go and **be with Christ, which would be far better for me**. But for your sakes, it is better that I continue to live. Knowing this, I am convinced that I will remain alive so I can continue to help all of you grow and experience the joy of your faith" (Phil. 1:21–25 NLT, boldface mine).

Hey, these are the words of a man who had power over life and death! It's far from some erroneous teachings I've heard from people, who tell you that "when your time comes," you will die and you have no say in the matter. I don't know what their Bibles say, but my Bible says, "With long life I will *satisfy you*" (see Ps. 91:16). All of us have a free choice to use our faith to believe God for a long life. How long a life? That depends on you—according to your faith and satisfaction be it unto you.

---

*All of us have a free choice to use our faith to believe God
for a long life.*

As for the apostle Paul, we know that he *was* satisfied before he was martyred because in the last chapter of his last epistle, he penned his epilogue: "For I am already being poured out as a drink offering, and the time of my departure is at hand. **I have fought the good fight, I have finished the race**, I have kept the faith. Finally, there is laid up for me the crown of righteousness" (2 Tim. 4:6–8, boldface mine). He decided that he had fought a good fight and had finished the race. It was enough; he was satisfied. We see here a man with authority over death. Paul was not murdered; he was ready to go.

Now, there were instances earlier in Paul's life when Paul was not yet ready to go. Once, when he was stoned, dragged out of the city of Lystra, and left for dead, do you know what he did? He got up, went back into the city, and continued preaching the gospel of grace (see Acts 14:19–21). Death had no hold on him! On another occasion, when he was on the island of Malta, a poisonous snake bit him while he was laying some wood he had gathered on a fire. Paul merely shook it off into the fire. The people who witnessed the snakebite waited for him to swell up or suddenly drop dead. But after they had waited for a long time and saw that he was completely unharmed, they decided that he was a god (see Acts 28:3–6 NLT). You and I know that the apostle Paul wasn't a god, but like you and I, he was a child of the Most High God. The serpent had no power over apostle Paul.

Dear reader, the same authority over the enemy that the apostle Paul had belongs to you and me today. Whatever the roaring lion or poisonous serpent is attacking you with today, remember, its rightful place is underneath your feet. Hallelujah!

10

PROTECTED BY THE FATHER'S LOVE

"Because he has set his love upon Me,
therefore I will deliver him;
I will set him on high, because he has known My name."
—Psalm 91:14

I want to start off this chapter by asking you a simple question: What qualifies you for God's protection?

I ask this question because I have heard many ministers whose teachings make it seem like you have to *qualify* for God's blessings. They make it sound like God blesses you *only* if you are able to love the Lord with all your heart, with all your soul, and with all your mind. This also applies in the area of your protection. When they read, "**Because** he has set his love upon Me, **therefore** I will deliver him" (boldface mine), they conclude that God's protection is dependent on us fulfilling the condition of loving the Lord perfectly.

Unfortunately, such teaching robs you of the faith to believe God for divine protection over yourself and your loved ones. Don't you agree that anything that is dependent on *our* efforts and *our* love for God is on a shaky foundation? No matter how "good" a Christian we think we are, our love for the Lord *will* fail.

The truth is, I personally don't know anyone who loves the Lord with all his or her heart, mind, and soul. Much as I wish otherwise, I know that I don't fulfill this requirement as well. That is precisely why God sent His Son. He knew that man would never be able to fulfill all His commandments. In sending His Son, He was saying to us, "I know you can't, so let *Me* love you with all My heart, all My mind, and all My strength." Therein lies the beautiful love story we call the gospel of Jesus Christ.

God SO loved the world that He sent His only begotten Son to save and ransom us. The Lord Jesus Christ Himself fulfilled *all* the requirements of the law. Today, even when our love for Him wavers, even when we fail, He still delivers us from evil!

Today, even when our love for Him wavers, He still delivers us from evil.

If there is one Scripture that encapsulates the crux of the new covenant of grace, it is this one: "In this is love, **not that we loved God, but that He loved us** and sent His Son *to be* the propitiation [the atoning sacrifice] for our sins" (1 John 4:10, boldface mine). I pray that your heart will be anchored on this revelation. The emphasis of the new covenant is God's love for you, not your love for God.

Am I saying that your love for God is unimportant? Of course not. What I am saying is that our love for Him will always waver, but His love *never* fails. The Bible declares that "the steadfast love of the Lord **never ceases**; his mercies never come to an end; they are new every morning" (Lam. 3:22–23 esv, boldface mine). I am so grateful that we are under the new covenant of God's amazing grace, where we can depend on *His* unconditional, unchanging, and irrevocable love for us!

The Cross Has Made a Difference

Under the old covenant, it is true that God's protection *was* conditional. But for you and me today, it is vital that we read and understand Psalm 91 through the lens of the new covenant—through the lens of the cross. We are no longer living under the old covenant. We have a new and living way (see Heb. 10:20)!

Under the old, protection is *achieved*. Under the new, protection is *received*. I have covered the differences between law and grace extensively in my other books like *Destined To Reign* and *Grace Revolution*, so I won't delve too deeply into this subject here. All I really want you to see is this: *The cross has made a difference.*

Under the old covenant, protection is achieved. *Under the new covenant, protection is* received. *The cross has made a difference.*

At the cross, God "made Him who knew no sin *to be* sin for us, that we might become the righteousness of God in Him" (2 Cor. 5:21). Today, we *are* the righteousness of God in Christ! Because we are righteous in Christ, we can receive the promise of Psalm 5:12, which declares, "For You, O Lord, will bless the righteous; with favor You will surround him as *with* a shield." Naturally, we can't always watch our backs. But supernaturally, God has got us covered all around. His abundant supply of grace (unmerited favor) encompasses us like a mighty and impenetrable force field, surrounding us 360 degrees and twenty-four hours a day!

God has got you covered—360 degrees,
twenty-four hours a day!

Set Your Mind on His Love

Coming back to the prayer of protection, how do we set our love upon God today? We set our love upon God by meditating on, talking about, and listening to preaching about His love for us! Remember, it is not about our love for Him, but His love for us. It is about us meditating on Bible verses like:

> *For God so greatly loved* and *dearly prized the world*
> *that He [even] gave up His only begotten (unique) Son,*
> *so that whoever believes in (trusts in, clings to, relies on)*
> *Him shall not perish (come to destruction, be lost) but*
> *have eternal (everlasting) life.*
>
> —*John 3:16* AMPC

There is protection and deliverance from destruction when you believe in God's love for you. Set your mind on how greatly loved and dearly prized you are. The more conscious you are of the Lord's love for you, the more His protection will manifest in your life!

Protected When You Put Your Trust in God

Daniel in the Old Testament is a good example of a man who set his mind on the Lord's love for him and experienced the Lord's deliverance. The Word of God tells us that Daniel had great favor with King Darius. Daniel proved himself to be more capable than all the other officials, and King Darius had a mind to make Daniel the prime minister over his entire empire. This stirred the jealousy of the other officials who did all they could to dig up some dirt on Daniel. But try as they might, Daniel was above reproach in every regard. They found him to be "faithful, always responsible, and completely trustworthy" (Dan. 6:4 NLT). The only snare they could devise was to point to Daniel's devotion to his God. (What a glorious accusation!)

They observed that without fail, Daniel would go to his upper room three times a day, get on his knees, and, with his windows open toward Jerusalem, pray and give thanks to his God. The conniving officials then tricked the king into signing a law decreeing that for thirty days, no one was to pray to anyone, divine or human, except to King Darius. If this decree was violated, the offender was to be thrown into a den of lions. They knew with certainty that Daniel would not stop praying to his God and could not wait to catch him. Sure enough, even after Daniel had heard about the new decree, he went up to his room and prayed to God just as he had always done.

The officials, who had gone to Daniel's house to catch him praying to God, went straight to King Darius. They reminded him of the law that he had signed and with mock chagrin accused Daniel of defying the king and his law. When the king heard their accusation, the Bible tells us that he was "greatly displeased," not with Daniel, but with himself because of his love for Daniel. For the rest of the day, he tried to find a way to save Daniel (see Dan. 6:14).

However, once an official law of the Medes and the Persians was issued, it could not be revoked. The king's hand was forced—he had no choice but to give the order for Daniel to be cast into the den of lions. The worried king spent the night fasting and refused his usual entertainment. Tossing and turning in his bed, he could not sleep at all. Very early the next morning, the king rushed to the lion's den. Read the account of what happened then:

> *When he got there, he called out in anguish, "Daniel, servant of the living God! Was your God, whom you serve so faithfully, able to rescue you from the lions?" Daniel answered, "Long live the king! My God sent his angel to shut the lions' mouths so that they would not hurt me, for I have been found innocent in his sight. And I have not wronged you, Your Majesty." The king was overjoyed and ordered that Daniel be lifted from the den.* **Not a scratch was found on him, for he had trusted in his God.**
>
> —*Daniel 6:20–23* NLT *(boldface mine)*

Now that you are more acquainted with Psalm 91, I am sure you can see many elements of the psalm in this account of God's deliverance. Daniel was clearly a man who dwelt daily in the secret place of the Most High, under the shadow of His wings. Daniel set his heart toward the Lord, praying and giving thanks to God three times a day. We also see one of God's angels in action and Daniel taking authority over fearsome, hungry lions within mere feet of him! In fact, he did not even suffer a single scratch after being shut up in a den full of lions for a whole night.

In contrast, when King Darius later ordered the officials who had schemed against Daniel to be thrown into the den, the lions "leaped on them and tore them apart before they even hit the floor of the den" (Dan. 6:24 NLT). Truly, the Lord was Daniel's refuge and fortress.

Seek the Protector

Now, depending on how established you are in God's grace, you can interpret Daniel's habit of praying three times a day as a religious routine, or you can see his dedicated prayer time as an outward expression of his intimate relationship with the Lord. Please be clear about this. I am not saying that if we want to be protected like Daniel, we have to pray three times a day. What I have really been saying throughout this book is that protection is *a result of closeness and intimacy* with the Lord.

Our experiencing God's protection is a result of closeness and intimacy with Him.

There are no formulas, steps, or shortcuts to walking in divine protection. Simply walk close with the Lord and you will unconsciously be under the shadow of His wings. Don't just pursue the protection, seek the Protector! You can recite Psalm 91 fifty times a day, but if you have no relationship with Jesus, there will be no results. The prayer of protection is not transactional; it is *relational*.

You've missed the point if you have to ask how many times a day you should pray. That is equivalent to asking your spouse, "How many times a day must I kiss you?" I wouldn't want my wife, Wendy, to ask me that! Relationships are birthed from the heart. They are not governed by formulas, rules, or algorithms. You kiss your spouse because of love. It is not an obligation; it is a privilege and pleasure. In the same way, don't mechanize your relationship with God. Every day, you can choose whether or not to meditate on His love for you. Daniel chose to do it three times a day. We can learn from that without turning it into a dry formula.

What Daniel had was an intimate *relationship* with the Lord. I pray that you will have this too. The Bible tells us that in his daily prayers, Daniel was always giving thanks to God. It is so good to live with thanksgiving in your heart toward the Lord. Each and every day, there are so many things that our Lord protects us from that we are not even aware of. Give thanks to Him for His love for you. Praise Him and set your mind daily toward Him. Be so conscious of how close you are to Him and how utterly loved you are—and enjoy the protection that comes from being found in the shadow of His wings!

Be so conscious of how close you are to the Lord and how utterly loved you are.

Protection in the Father

Can I show you a beautiful picture of God's love for you found in the story of Daniel? We saw how in Daniel's case, the law of the land was violated and how, in spite of his love for Daniel, the king had to carry out the law and punish Daniel. If he hadn't, he would have been an unrighteous king. Now, imagine if someone came again a year later to accuse Daniel of this crime and asked for Daniel to be punished again, what would the king do? Would the king throw Daniel into the lion's den again? No! Daniel had already been sentenced; he had already paid the price for his violation of the law.

My dear friend, because our Lord Jesus has been punished on the cross in your place, the devil cannot come to the King and ask for you to be punished and thrown into the lion's den. You see, your sins were forgiven not because the King simply decided to close an eye and let you off the hook. The King forgave your sins *righteously* after judging them in the body of our Lord Jesus Christ. He who was completely without sin took your place and bore the full weight of the punishment for your sins (see 2 Cor. 5:21). ALL your sins have been legally and judicially judged at the cross. Because of His finished work, once you received the Lord Jesus into your heart, God's justice and righteousness are on your side!

Do you know how much God loves Jesus, His beloved Son and the apple of His eye? Then I pray that you will have a revelation of how much your Father in heaven loves YOU. To redeem you, God paid the price with the blood of His only Son. It must have been a most difficult decision for Him. None of us would ever fully comprehend what God experienced in sending His own beloved Son to the cross. We catch just a small glimpse of the torment that God suffered when we read about King Darius's suffering. King Darius wanted to save Daniel, but he could not violate his own law. Similarly, God loves His Son, but He knew the only way to save us, who had violated the law, was to sacrifice His own Son, Jesus Christ.

Knowing His Name

Psalm 91:14 says, "I will set him on high, because he has known **My name**" (boldface mine). We have talked about seeing the names of God in just the first two verses of Psalm 91 alone, and how that brings revelation and comfort to us. Yet, did you know that Jesus came to reveal only one name?

Our Lord Jesus came to reveal the name "Father." *Father* speaks of family and of closeness and intimacy. You can know God as *Elyon*, the Most High. As *El Shaddai*, God Almighty. As *Yehovah*, the Lord, the covenant-keeping God. As *Elohim*, mighty Creator of the heavens and the earth. Every name is so significant as each one reveals a wonderful aspect of our God. But when you know God as *Father*, *all* His virtues, attributes, and power work *for* you to set you on high and deliver you.

When you know God as Father, all His virtues, attributes, and power work for you to set you on high and deliver you.

Our Lord Jesus prayed, "Now I am no longer in the world, but these are in the world, and I come to You. Holy Father, keep through Your name those whom You have given Me, that they may be one as We *are*" (John 17:11). The Greek word for "keep" here is the word *tereo*, which means to attend to carefully, to take care of, to guard, to watch, and to preserve.[1] What is the name through which you will be kept guarded and protected? FATHER. Beloved, I want you to know beyond the shadow of a doubt that you have a heavenly Father who loves you, who gave up His all for you, and who is vigilantly watching over you!

Do you want to see how having a revelation of your Father's love for you can keep and preserve you? Let me end this chapter by sharing with you a glorious testimony from a professional athlete who attends our church in Dallas:

> *My wife and I have been attending Grace Revolution Church in Dallas, Texas. It has truly been a year of greater glory in every area of our lives—our marriage, finances, career, and physical bodies. One of the many demonstrations of His amazing love came not long ago.*
>
> *One Saturday evening, as I was preparing for bed, I noticed that my left testicle was enlarged and hard. I decided to make an appointment to see our family doctor first thing on Monday morning, as I knew that something was not right. I began to be worried and fearful.*
>
> *But at church the next morning, I felt the Lord encouraging me through Pastor Prince's broadcast message. I was also prayed over and anointed with oil. When Monday came, my wife and I went to the doctor in a state of peace as we rested in our Father's love.*
>
> *After I had an ultrasound and a consultation with a urologist, I was diagnosed with testicular cancer. But despite the doctor's report, we chose to cling to the report of the Lord. We knew our heavenly Father would guide us in the decisions we needed to make and we sensed an overwhelming peace in the midst of the storm. We felt so at rest in the finished work of Jesus and*

were filled with an unexplainable joy. We believed that just as Jesus is, so was I in my physical body.

The doctor wanted to move forward with surgery that Thursday to remove the mass in the left testicle. That would be followed up with a computerized tomography (CT) scan on Friday to assess what further treatment would be needed. During the consultation, we felt very restful about moving forward with the surgery and decided to schedule the procedure, believing that I was already healed because of Jesus' finished work. We also continually reminded ourselves of our righteousness in Him as we partook of the Holy Communion daily.

On Thursday, the surgery went very well. However, after the surgery, the doctor spoke to my wife with much concern, as the cancerous mass was very large and belonged to the mixed germ cell tumor category. Despite the doctor's concern, my wife and I continued to believe that I was completely free of cancer in my body.

On Friday morning, I went in for another CT scan to see if the cancer had spread to the nearby areas. I went in believing that I was healed and that nothing would be found. When the doctor looked over the report, he was astounded. The CT scan confirmed that I was completely cancer-free and extremely healthy.

The doctor found the report very shocking because his experience had taught him that cancer cells of the size and type that I had would certainly have spread to the surrounding areas. He had actually already made an appointment for me to see a specialist to discuss the options for chemotherapy and radiation *therapy even before the CT scan. However, after looking at the report, he agreed that it was no longer necessary and canceled the appointment!*

The doctor was very pleased to see how quickly I recovered and was able to return to my normal activities. The surgery took place right in the midst of my off-season training program, which meant there were no setbacks in my training whatsoever. This was important to me as a professional athlete.

My wife and I know that our heavenly Father had protected me and kept the cancer contained, and subsequently had it removed. What the enemy tried to use as a setback, our heavenly Father used as a divine set-up. Now, as I share this story with people I cross paths with, I am able to use it as a glorious testimony of the health and wholeness that we have in Jesus. Through the whole experience, my wife and I were able to remain at rest because we knew that the Father sees us as righteous through His Son, Jesus, and we are completely loved by Him.

Glory to God!

Wow. Glory to God indeed! There is such power in knowing that the all-powerful, almighty God of Israel is not someone far away. He paid the price so that you and I could *draw near* to Him. Joseph in the book of Genesis wanted his family to dwell in Goshen, which means "drawing near."[2] He wanted them in a place of nearness to him and he told them, "There **I will provide** for you" (Gen. 45:11, boldface mine).

Beloved, even in the midst of famine, Jesus, our heavenly Joseph, wants us close to Him so He can provide for us. In the book of

Exodus, God declared, "I will **set apart the land of Goshen**, in which My people dwell, that no swarms *of flies* shall be there" (Exod. 8:22, boldface mine). In the land of Goshen, God's people were protected from all of the ten plagues that besieged the land of Egypt during the time of Moses. In the second last of the ten plagues, a thick, paralyzing darkness covered the land of Egypt for three whole days. Yet, during that time, "**all the children of Israel had light in their dwellings**" (Exod. 10:23, boldface mine).

Even in the midst of famine, our Lord Jesus wants to provide for us.

I believe it was a supernatural darkness that covered Egypt, because the Egyptians, who would have had more access to natural resources of light than the Israelite slaves, must have turned to those resources to dispel the darkness—only to find they couldn't. By the same token, it was a supernatural light that the Israelites enjoyed in Goshen, a light the darkness tried to smother but couldn't.

Now, I believe this is prophetic of our times. The Bible is relevant for today. We are living in days where we see darkness—a supernatural darkness—cover the earth. Yet, the Scriptures tell us that even when there's thick and deep darkness all around, the church—you and I, together with our families—can experience and enjoy God's supernatural light in our dwellings. We, who have been drawn near to Him through the work of His Son, can have intimacy with God and enjoy His protective covering to live fear-free and victoriously in these dark times.

*Even when there's deep darkness all around, you and I can
enjoy God's supernatural light in our dwellings.*

Beloved, in the place of nearness, God makes a difference between His people and the people of the world. We are in this world, but we are not of this world (see John 17:14). We are His. He desires for us to be close to Him so that He can hide us under the shadow of His wings. He paid the price so that we can be called His children. Oh, what manner of love the Father has given unto us, that we should be called the sons and daughters of the Most High (see 1 John 3:1)!

He is your Father. Your Daddy. Your Abba.

That is the name by which He wants you to call Him. When my son, Justin, has a nightmare, he doesn't call out, "Pastor Prince!" He just cries out, "Abba!" and I am there, ready to take on any monsters hiding under his bed. In the same way, you can have complete assurance that when you call upon your Father, He *will* answer you. You can have full confidence in your Father's protection and deliverance for you and your family, not because of your love for Him, but because of *His* love for you.

Beloved, whatever may be happening in the world today, you can be bold and fearless because nothing can ever separate you from the love of God, your heavenly Father. As the Word of God proclaims in Romans 8:38–39, "Neither death nor life, nor angels nor principalities nor powers, nor things present nor things to come, nor height nor depth, nor any other created thing, shall be able to separate us from the love of God which is in Christ Jesus our Lord"!

II

WISDOM TO
STAY SAFE

"He shall call upon Me, and I will answer him;
I will be with him in trouble;
I will deliver him and honor him."
—*Psalm 91:15*

We have a God who wants us to run to Him. And the moment we do, He has promised that He *will* answer us. Not "might," or "perhaps," but a definite "will." And He does not stop at merely assuring us that He will answer us. He goes on record for all eternity, saying, "I *will be* with him in trouble; I **will** deliver him and honor him" (boldface mine).

Do you know why we can have the assurance that when we call on Him, He will answer us? It's because of the divine exchange that took place at the cross, where our Lord Jesus cried out, "My God, My God, why have You forsaken Me?" (Matt. 27:46). He was forsaken—left helpless, totally abandoned, and deserted—so that today, we can have the confidence that our heavenly Father will never leave us nor forsake us (see Heb. 13:5).

What a Savior!

Don't you feel so loved and so cherished by our Lord? We have a Savior who loves us, not one who is distant and indifferent. And He made it so easy for us to receive His promises—our part is to simply *call upon Him* and to let Him be our God. He desires to have an intimate relationship with us and He loves it when we acknowledge our need for Him, and allow Him to hide us under the shadow of His wings and hold us close to His heart of love. Whatever you may be going through today, call upon Him right now and He will deliver and honor you!

God loves it when we acknowledge our need for Him,
and allow Him to hide us under the shadow of His wings.

Whenever I am troubled, I tell the Lord, "Lord, I am worried about this situation, but I place it in Your nail-pierced hands right now. I surrender into Your hands all my worries, concerns, and cares in this area." Then, I receive His peace, and when the enemy tries to fire new arrows of fear into my heart and mind, I remind myself that the situation is already in the Lord's hands. I remind myself of His promise that He will deliver me!

Are you living with panic attacks, fear, and chronic anxiety? Don't allow the devil to cripple you with all kinds of negative mental pictures, or by replaying all the worst-case scenarios in your head. Call out to your Savior, Jesus Christ! He wants you to cast "**all** your care upon Him, **for He cares for you**" (1 Pet. 5:7, boldface mine). You are not a sheep without a Shepherd, so stop trying to carry all your cares upon your own shoulders.

Whether it is a physical symptom, a financial challenge, or a family situation that you are anxious about, call upon Him and allow His peace to supernaturally guard your heart in every area that you are troubled. The Bible says, "Be anxious for nothing, but in everything by prayer and supplication, with thanksgiving, let your

requests be made known to God; and the peace of God, which surpasses all understanding, will guard your hearts and minds through
Christ Jesus" (Phil. 4:6–7).

A Very Present Help in Trouble

I want to share a portion of this beautiful psalm with you:

> *God* is *our refuge and strength,*
> *A very present help in trouble.*
> *Therefore we will not fear,*
> *Even though the earth be removed,*
> *And though the mountains be carried into*
>   *the midst of the sea;*
> Though *its waters roar* and *be troubled,*
> Though *the mountains shake with its swelling.*
> —*Psalm 46:1–3*

We do not need to fear—even in times
of trouble, Jesus is our very present help, our refuge,
and our strength.

What a powerful promise! We do not need to fear because even in
times of turmoil and trouble, He is our very present help, our refuge,
and our strength! Our part is to call upon Him and He will answer

and deliver us. Melinda, a lady from our church, experienced this for herself and wrote to me to share her testimony:

Early one Monday morning, I was driving my six-year-old son to school. As I exited the freeway, I approached a traffic light junction with heavy traffic. At that time, my son and I were listening to Pastor Prince's sermon CD in the car and I was amazed by how God had saved Noah and his family from the flood. Suddenly, I heard a loud bang as something hit the back of my car. The next thing I knew, my car was flung into the air. It overturned, landed on its roof, and spun a distance to a halt.

As the car was spinning, I knew we were in a serious accident. I knew in my heart that if we crashed into anything we could be dead or badly injured. I started screaming, "Jesus!" at least five times until the car finally came to a halt. As I was screaming, my hands were holding on to the steering wheel tightly. I could not even hold my boy. I could only turn my head to look at him.

He was sitting beside me that morning. His body was miraculously held to the contour of the seat. Even though we were spinning upside down and he only had a seat belt strapped across his body, his head and legs were not dangling from his seat. His neck could have been broken from the impact of the crash, but he was okay. While seat belts are important, I knew that it was Jesus who hugged us tightly and saved our lives!

My first instinct was to get out, as I feared a petrol leak, which could result in an explosion. So I unbuckled the both of us and opened my door. My son and I crawled out of the wreck without a scratch or whiplash. We stood by the side of the road and a lot of passersby came to our aid. The small car that had crashed into our car was speeding so fast that after sending us flying, it screeched ahead and barreled into another black car and an orange bus. The entire accident caused a massive traffic jam that morning.

After we had gotten out of the car wreck, the picture of Jesus bleeding on the cross kept flashing in my mind. I knew that my son and I didn't have to bleed on the road that morning because Jesus had shed His blood for us.

After regaining my composure, I went back to my wrecked car to get my bag and my son's schoolbag with the help of some passersby. Pastor Prince's message was still playing loudly although the car was in such a bad state.

Someone wanted to take my car key out but I told him there was no need to. The car was already a wreck and I saw no point in keeping the key. I wanted God's Word to be played so that everyone who was present would know that Jesus is the One who saved our lives. That morning, it was effortless and restful to be a witness for the glory of God. I told everyone who came to our aid that Jesus had saved us.

Though unharmed, we were urged to follow the ambulance to get a checkup. The driver of the black car that was hit was in a worse state than us, even though our car was more badly damaged than his.

When my husband came to meet us at the hospital, he shared with us that he had also been driving to work around *the time of the car accident, and how he felt prompted by the Holy Spirit to switch off the radio and pray in tongues. He also confessed the Lord's favor over our lives, something that we had learned in church the day before. I believe the Lord must have prompted him to pray for us during the time of the car accident.*

Later in the day, a lady who had stopped to help us at the accident scene called to thank me even though I thought I should be the one thanking her! She told me that she and her husband had been struggling spiritually in recent months. But they were very blessed by what she saw and heard (Pastor Prince's message playing from the car).

On Friday, my husband and I went to collect the wrecked car for assessment. The car was in such a sorry state, yet my son and I came out unscathed. As we were checking the car, I realized that all the doors but one were jammed and could not be opened. The only door that could be opened was the one we had instinctively used to get out. All glory to Jesus!

My family and I are recovering well from the shock and trauma of the accident. I have even started driving again. After what happened, what more is there to fear? Jesus turned a possibly tragic accident into a victorious outcome. No amount of safe driving could have saved our lives, only Jesus and nothing else!

Praise the Lord! In her time of trouble, Melinda cried out the name of Jesus and He answered her. No matter what situation we are in, the Lord is with us and will surely deliver us when we call upon His name!

---

*Whatever our situation, the Lord is with us and will
surely deliver us when we call upon His name.*

Jesus Is with Us in Our Troubles

The book of Daniel records how King Nebuchadnezzar of Babylon made a towering golden statue and commanded all in his kingdom to bow down before it and worship it. Three young men, Shadrach, Meshach, and Abednego, whom the king had appointed to oversee the province of Babylon, refused to do so. Humiliated by their defiance, the king was livid. He gave them one more chance to bow down and worship his golden statue or be thrown immediately into a blazing furnace.

Without flinching, they said, "O Nebuchadnezzar, we do not need to defend ourselves before you. If we are thrown into the blazing furnace, the God whom we serve is able to save us. He will rescue us from your power, Your Majesty. But even if he doesn't...we will never serve your gods or worship the gold statue you have set up" (Dan. 3:16–18 NLT). The king was so furious with them that his face became distorted with rage. He commanded that the furnace be heated seven times hotter than usual, and ordered some of his strongest soldiers to bind them and throw them into the furnace. The furnace was so hot that the flames killed the soldiers as they threw the three men in. Shadrach, Meshach, and Abednego fell into the roaring flames, securely bound.

Suddenly, the king jumped up in amazement and exclaimed to his officials, "Did we not cast three men bound into the midst of the fire?" They answered and said to the king, "True, O king." "Look!" he answered, "I see four men loose, walking in the midst of the fire; and they are not hurt, and the form of the fourth is like the Son of God" (Dan. 3:24–25). Going as close to the mouth of the flaming furnace as he could, Nebuchadnezzar called out, "Shadrach, Meshach, and Abednego, servants of the Most High God, come out! Come here!" The three men stepped out of the fire and all the officials and advisers crowded around them and "saw that the fire had not touched them. Not a hair on their heads was singed, and their clothing was not scorched" (Dan. 3:26–27 NLT). In fact, the flames only served to loose them from their bonds.

Amazed at how their God had protected them, Nebuchadnezzar began praising God himself, saying, "Blessed be the God of Shadrach, Meshach, and Abed-Nego, who sent His Angel and delivered His servants who trusted in Him" (Dan. 3:28). The king then issued a decree stating that if any person spoke a word against the God of Shadrach, Meshach, and Abednego, they would be cut in pieces and their houses would be turned into ash heaps "because there is no other God who can deliver like this" (Dan. 3:29). Then, the king promoted the three men to even higher positions in the province of Babylon.

Beloved, this is *your* God.

There is truly no other god who can rescue like Him. Whatever circumstances you might be thrown into, our Lord Jesus is the fourth man with you *in the midst* of the fire. Notice how He didn't stand outside of the fire, but was in the fire together with the three friends. This brings a whole new meaning for us when we read the verse, "Be strong and of good courage, do not fear nor be afraid of them; for the LORD your God, He *is* the One who **goes with you**. He will not leave you nor forsake you" (Deut. 31:6, boldface mine). Our Lord doesn't deliver you from afar; He is with you in the midst of your adversity. Call upon Him and He will answer you. When Jesus is with you, nothing can harm you!

Our Lord doesn't deliver you from afar; He is with you in the midst of your adversity.

Don't you just love how the Word of God describes the three friends when they came out of the furnace? They were in the fire, but it had absolutely no power over them. It did not even leave a trace of smoke on them! Now, that's a beautiful picture of God's divine protection!

Beloved, as you call upon the Lord in your day of trouble, my prayer for you is that the trial you are going through will have no power over you; it will not even leave a smell on you. Instead, I declare in Jesus' name that you will walk out of that challenge in your life and the only smell on you will be the fragrance of the Lord Jesus (see 2 Cor. 2:14)! As the people around you witness how the Lord delivers you, may they come to know His wonderful name and give Him praise. Instead of being negatively affected by whatever trial you might face, I pray that you will receive honor and promotion just like Shadrach, Meshach, and Abednego. Amen!

Walk in Wisdom to Stay Safe

It gives me such assurance to know that the Lord can deliver us from trouble. But do you know what's better than being delivered from trouble?

Not *getting* into trouble in the first place.

My dear reader, don't just seek miracles and protection from God without seeking the wisdom from Him to stay protected and out of trouble. There are times when the challenges that we face are beyond our control. But I've found that often, we experience His protection when we follow the Holy Spirit and lean on His wisdom when making decisions. Every day, we need His wisdom, just as we need His protection. After all, Proverbs 4:7 tells us that "wisdom *is* the principal thing," and in all our getting, we need to *get wisdom*.

Don't just seek miracles and protection from God without seeking His wisdom to stay out of trouble.

The Bible tells us that Christ has become for us wisdom from God (see 1 Cor. 1:30). So what we really need is the Lord Jesus. We need to lean on Him and draw close to Him daily. He is our wisdom and only He can cause us to always be at the right place at the right time. I believe that many troubles and dangerous situations can be completely avoided when we don't depend on our own wisdom and planning, but involve the Lord in all that we do (see Prov. 3:6).

*Christ is our wisdom and only He can cause us to always
be at the right place at the right time.*

Oftentimes, wisdom and divine protection work hand in hand. Knowing that we can trust God for His protection certainly does not mean that we should willfully put ourselves in precarious situations. We need to apply wisdom and heed the Lord's leading through the wise counsel of the people around us, such as our leaders in the local church and our spouses. Proverbs 11:14 tells us, "Where *there is* no counsel, the people fall; but in the multitude of counselors *there is* safety." For instance, if your spouse has been telling you that you have a problem with speeding, please take heed. While there can be divine protection, do not be foolish and think that you can do whatever you want and nothing untoward will ever happen to you.

Our Lord Jesus demonstrated this to us Himself. When the devil tried to tempt Him to jump off the pinnacle of the temple, quoting Scripture to say that angels were supposed to bear Him up, our Lord Jesus responded by saying, "The Scriptures also say, 'You must not test the Lord your God'" (Matt. 4:7 NLT). Likewise, let us not test the Lord by making irresponsible and unwise decisions that ignore the godly counsel spoken over our lives.

When you are led by His wisdom, the Lord can protect you from making unwise decisions. For example, someone may offer you "the investment opportunity of a lifetime." On the surface, everything might seem to check out and it may appear to be a legitimate opportunity that is not to be missed. But before you rush to commit to anything, can I encourage you to first ask the Lord for His wisdom and leading?

Before you rush to commit to anything, ask the Lord for His wisdom and leading.

There is a principle we can learn from in Isaiah 11, where it says of the Lord that "the spirit of wisdom and understanding" will rest on Him, and "He will not judge by what His eyes see, nor make a decision by what His ears hear" (Isa. 11:2–3 NASB). You see, there is a discernment and wisdom from the Lord that goes beyond looking at the outward appearance of a matter. When you call on Him, He will answer you and give you an answer of peace. If you don't feel a peace to proceed, don't allow anyone to pressure you into making a decision you will regret!

Be Led by the Holy Spirit

The more areas of your life you involve the Lord in, the more you can experience His protection. You can even ask the Lord to guide you in something as seemingly natural as your travel itinerary. In fact, that's what apostle Paul did. Look at the account of how he allowed the Holy Spirit to lead them at every step:

> *Now when they had gone through Phrygia and the region of Galatia, they were forbidden by the Holy*

> *Spirit to preach the word in Asia. After they had come to*
> *Mysia, they tried to go into Bithynia, but the Spirit did*
> *not permit them.*
>
> —*Acts 16:6–7*

We see from the above Scriptures that closed doors are not necessarily negative, and could be signs of God's protection over our lives. The challenge for some of us is that we are so adept at planning and scheduling our busy lives that many times, we don't make room for the Lord to intervene and to guide us to be at the right place at the right time. Let's not put our trust in our intelligence and planning, but in His wisdom, leading, and counsel. There is a proverb that says, "A man's heart plans his way, but the LORD directs his steps" (Prov. 16:9). Even as we plan, I pray that we will always remember to commit all our ways to the Lord, and allow *Him* to direct our steps.

Let's not put our trust in our intelligence and planning,
but in His wisdom and counsel.

Being led by the Spirit does not have to be something complicated. When you walk close to the Lord and have a close relationship with Him, He can lead you in supernaturally natural ways. Some years ago, a couple in our church shared with our leaders how they were vacationing at a beach resort on Penang Island in Malaysia, when the wife felt like eating something in another location on the mainland, some distance away. Because of that "prompting" in her belly, they packed their things and headed off earlier than they had originally planned to. While they were loading up their vehicle, there was a man who kept hurrying them and asking them to move off as they were apparently blocking the hotel driveway, and that had really irritated them at that time.

In any case, they headed off, and just fifteen minutes after they had crossed the border from the island to the mainland, they heard the news that an earthquake in the Indian Ocean had triggered a killer tsunami that crashed onto the beachfront they were at, killing more than fifty people. Had they left just a little later, they could have been among the casualties of the tragedy that day. Looking back, the couple believes that the man at the hotel might even have been an angel sent by the Lord to get them out of harm's way quickly.

I don't know about you, but I want the Lord to direct *all* my steps! Call upon Him today and He will answer you.

12

GOD'S PROMISE OF LONG LIFE

"With long life I will satisfy him,
And show him My salvation."
—*Psalm 91:16*

We have come to the final but, I think, most important verse in Psalm 91! Praise the Lord, you've stayed the course with this book, and I pray that you have been greatly blessed and enriched. My dear friend, if you ever had any doubt that God desires for you to live a long, good life, let this verse be your answer. You may be battling with a health condition right now, but by faith let's hold fast to this verse together. In Jesus' mighty name, I see you healed, healthy, and whole. I see you strong in Christ and ready to take on any giant that is ahead of you.

One of my favorite pictures of long life is found in the biblical character Caleb. Let me quote what he said when he was eighty-five years old: "I am this day, eighty-five years old. As yet I *am as* strong this day as on the day that Moses sent me; just as my strength *was* then, so now *is* my strength for war, both for going out and for coming in" (Josh. 14:10–11).

Did you hear that? Caleb was eighty-five years old when he said that! How old are you again? You are young, my friend. And the faith picture here of long life is not just in terms of *quantity*—the number of days—but also *quality*—health and strength. Caleb lived long and remained strong. He wasn't just strong *for* an eighty-five-year-old. That would've been pretty good already, wouldn't you say? But the Bible says Caleb was as strong at eighty-five as he was when he was forty-five. Which means in the last forty years in the harsh wilderness, his strength, youth, and vigor didn't diminish. There was no leaking, no receding, and no fading away of his strength!

That is pretty astounding. And if perhaps you think that Caleb was just a grumpy old man blowing hot air and talking big, look at what he said next:

> *"Now therefore, give me this mountain of which the LORD spoke in that day; for you heard in that day how the Anakim were there, and that the cities were great and fortified. It may be that the LORD will be with me, and I shall be able to drive them out as the LORD said."*
>
> *—Joshua 14:12*

Do you hear that? At eighty-five, Caleb was not ready to pack it up and slow down. He was ready to pick a fight with *giants* to gain possession of a mountain! And again this was not just some trash-talking babble; Caleb did as he said! Read the evidence for yourself: "And Joshua blessed him, and gave Hebron to Caleb the son of Jephunneh as an inheritance. Hebron therefore became the inheritance of Caleb the son of Jephunneh the Kenizzite to this day, because he wholly followed the LORD God of Israel" (Josh. 14:13–14).

You were impressed when a teenage shepherd boy picked a fight with one giant named Goliath in the valley of Elah? I think we should be completely blown away by this eighty-five-year-old, who took on a *whole mountain* packed with giants! For Caleb, it wasn't an issue of personal pride or accomplishment. He was zealous for the Lord's glory. As far as Caleb was concerned, there was unfinished business because the Lord had promised them the mountain forty years ago. My personal belief is that his biological clock stopped ticking and he basically stopped aging because he kept his eyes not on himself, but on the promises of the Lord.

Follow the Lord

What are your eyes fixed on today? Are they focused on the darkness that is in the world? Or are they fixed on the Lord's promises for your life? My chief intention in this book has been to turn your eyes away from the destruction you see every day, and to turn them to our beautiful Lord Jesus.

The secret to long life is found in simply
following the Lord.

Do you know what Caleb's secret to long life was? Joshua 14:14 records that "Hebron therefore became the inheritance of Caleb… because he **wholly followed** the LORD God of Israel" (boldface mine). His secret to long life was found in simply *following* the Lord. Do you remember the meaning for the name "Hebron"? It was the name for one of the cities of refuge we talked about in chapter 7. In Hebrew, "Hebron" means fellowship or association. This speaks of intimacy, closeness, and connection with the Lord.

There is no formula to long life. The prayer of protection is not a mantra. What we have been talking about throughout this book all point back to the importance of having an intimate relationship with Jesus. Our Lord Jesus is the way, the truth, and the life. He came that we might have life and have it more abundantly. *Follow* Him and find the path to a long and abundant life. Don't forget that everything Caleb experienced was under the old covenant. His renewal of youth and unabated strength and vigor were all experienced under the old covenant. *How much more* should we be experiencing this renewal of youth, boundless energy, and length of days under the new covenant of grace that is established on better promises (see Heb. 8:6)! Amen!

In a psalm that Moses wrote, it says, "The days of our lives *are* seventy years; and if by reason of strength *they are* eighty years" (Ps. 90:10). Some people have used this to teach that our expected lifespan is therefore between seventy and eighty years. But it is important we interpret this psalm in the context of the children of Israel being in the wilderness and under God's wrath. We have also seen that even under the old covenant, Caleb transcended this lifespan and was still going strong at eighty-five years old.

So dear reader—you who are under the new covenant—I encourage you to aim high. Don't settle for living till just seventy or eighty years old, when God has promised, "With long life I will **satisfy him,** and show him My salvation" (Ps 91:16, boldface mine). *Your satisfaction* is the limit and according to your faith, be it unto you. I pray that as you stay close to our Lord Jesus, you will live long, live strong, and live under the protective covering of His wings.

As you stay close to our Lord Jesus, you will live long, live strong, and live under the protective covering of His wings.

Salvation in the Name of Jesus

Psalm 91 ends with the power-packed verse, "With long life I will satisfy him, and show him My salvation." Many years ago, the Lord opened my eyes to see that apart from the four names of God that we covered in the first two verses of Psalm 91, there is another name of God, a fifth name, hidden in this psalm. I had never heard anyone preach this before so it was very exciting for me when He showed me His name, concealed in the very last word of Psalm 91.

You see, in Hebrew, the word "salvation" is the word *yeshua*.[1] And *Yeshua* is the Hebrew name of our Lord Jesus! Now, isn't that beautiful? This is what God was saying: "With long life I will satisfy him, and show him My *Yeshua*." Long life is found in our *Yeshua*. You can know God as *El Elyon*, God Most High, as the Almighty *Shaddai*, as *Jehovah*, and even as *Elohim*, but the name that gives you full and utter confidence is the name Jesus!

It is not enough to know that God is all-powerful. It is more important you know that God is willing to use His power and might to *save you*! That's what our Lord Jesus did at the cross for you and me. He came and He showed us His salvation by sacrificing Himself on the cross for your sins and my sins. *He died young that we may live long.* And not just live long in this world. At the cross, He purchased for us the gift of eternal life, paid for with His own blood.

The moment you received Jesus as your Lord and Savior, your salvation in Him was sure and secure!

Our Lord Jesus died young that we may live long.

I grew up in a church where I was taught that when you sin, you will lose your salvation and have to get born again all over again. This erroneous teaching oppressed my mind day and night. The enemy incessantly attacked me with thoughts that I had lost my salvation. As I was seeking the Lord for answers one day, He opened my eyes and pointed me to 2 Timothy 4:18: "And the Lord will deliver me from **every evil work** and preserve *me* for His heavenly kingdom" (boldface mine).

Just like that, when the truth of God's Word came in, all the oppression left me. And every time the thought that I had lost my salvation reared its ugly head again, I would quote this verse, boldly declaring, "It is written, 'And the Lord will deliver me from every evil work and preserve me for His heavenly kingdom.'" Beloved, if you are looking for a New Testament Scripture on protection to meditate upon, I highly recommend this Scripture written by the apostle Paul. In this one verse you find the Lord's protection and preservation unto eternity!

Worship the Lord

I am sure that you have heard a lot of teaching on fearing the Lord. I do believe in a reverential honor of the Lord. But I am not for any kind of teaching that promotes this idea that God wants you to be afraid of Him. Throughout this entire book, I have shown you how much God delights in having us *close* to Him. He welcomes us to dwell in His secret place, to be so close to Him that we come under His shadow. These are all pictures of intimacy. In any relationship, fear and intimacy cannot coexist. If you fear God today, you won't be able to believe Him for His protection. That is why it is so important for you to be strong and established in His grace.

God welcomes us to draw so close to Him that we come under His shadow.

The author of the book of Hebrews says, "Let us therefore come boldly to the throne of grace, that we may obtain mercy and find grace to help in time of need" (Heb. 4:16). This is a picture of the ark of the covenant (which we've covered in chapter 4), God's throne of grace. Because our Lord's blood has been shed on the mercy seat, today, we can come boldly into His presence without any sense of inferiority or shame, and receive His favor, His supply, His protection, and His help in our time of need.

Do you know how Jesus defined the fear of the Lord? He defined it as the *worship* of the Lord. (I touched on this in chapter 8, but this is a revelation that bears repeating because it's so important.) In the wilderness temptation, when the devil brought our Lord to a high mountain and showed Him all the kingdoms of the world and their glory, he said to Jesus, "All these things I will give You if You will fall down and worship me." Jesus then replied, "Away with you, Satan! For it is written, 'You shall worship the LORD your God, and Him only you shall serve'" (Matt. 4:8–10). Our Lord was quoting from Deuteronomy 6:13, which says, "You shall fear the LORD your God and serve Him." Did you see how our Lord substituted the word "fear" with the word "worship"?

Jesus was showing us how to accurately understand the fear of the Lord. In the new covenant, it has nothing to do with being afraid of the Lord; it has everything to do with coming into His presence with boldness and worshiping Him. Stop living in fear, my friend. Instead, follow our Lord wholly like Caleb did and worship His wonderful name. The prayer of protection is a psalm of worship. When you worship Jesus, all your fears will fade away. When you worship Him, the angel of the Lord encamps around you like a shield of protection. When you worship your Savior, His Spirit of wisdom and counsel will lead and guide you with rivers of peace!

When you worship Jesus, all your fears will fade away.

A lady from Virginia wrote to share with me her testimony of how following the leading of the Lord guided and protected her and her daughters while they were on a road trip. Be blessed as you see how practical the Lord was in looking after all their needs and keeping them safe:

> *I just wanted to share what the Lord has done for us in the area of protection.*

In one of your messages of the year, you mentioned that we needed the Lord's protection. I listened to that message over and over again, and confessed that we were crowned with the Lord's glory and honor.

In April, my two daughters and I went on a road trip from Virginia to Georgia and experienced one of the biggest tornado outbreaks in US history. A few days before we left for the trip, I had the urge to just read Psalm 91 and Psalm 23 again with my children. *We read the Scriptures and quoted verses out loud, and then I read it again to my girls as they drifted off to sleep.*

On the day of the trip itself, we encountered horrendous storms with awfully dark clouds, torrential winds, and hail as we drove through Virginia and Tennessee. In my heart, I felt that I needed to just drive through the storms and did so by God's grace.

We stopped to eat in north Georgia. I wanted to hurry and eat so that we could get back on the road quickly. But in my heart, I felt the Lord telling me to slow down *and let my girls eat and relax, and not to rush them.*

When we left the restaurant, I felt the urge to get gas at the gas station next door. *I didn't know why because my gas tank was already more than half full. But I did it anyway. Then, we got back on the highway and continued our trip.*

After traveling less than a mile, the traffic came to a complete stop. We waited for a while and then realized that something serious had just happened right up ahead.

A large tornado had just torn through the town directly in front of us only minutes before! It had traveled and caused destruction on the very section of the highway that we were going to travel on. By God's grace, the Lord had us stop to get food and gas, slowing us down enough to keep us from the destructive tornado! We missed the tornado by only three to five minutes.

We were stuck on the highway for five hours as emergency crews began to emerge from everywhere to help the victims of the tornado. We prayed in the Spirit for the victims and sang praises to the Lord for His saving grace.

Although we were in the car and couldn't move for five hours, we now had enough gas in our car to keep the DVD playing (for the girls) for most of the five hours. The Lord had prepared us for this without me even knowing it. When packing for the trip, I had packed extra water, food, blankets, DVDs, and more for the girls.

While we waited in the car, another storm arose and traveled over us. It shook our SUV violently and all those on the radio said that another tornado was imminent. We were stuck on the highway with no way to exit. The exit up ahead had been torn apart by the tornado before.

I began to confess Psalm 91 over us and told my daughters that the Lord would keep us safe no matter what the storm looked like. The Word of God calmed our hearts. We turned off the bad news on the radio and just sang praises to God for His protection, and He protected us. Amazingly, the second storm didn't produce another tornado! The Lord kept us safe and I am so thankful!

The devil intended to cause destruction in our lives but the Lord's amazing power, love, and grace made sure that we were always held safe and warm in the secret place of the Most High.

> *Thank you so much for preaching the true gospel of Jesus Christ. God bless and keep you and your family!*

Don't you just love how the Lord led this family in such specific ways by getting them to read the psalm of protection, stay longer at that restaurant, and even to top up on gas? When we follow Him and allow Him to lead us, the Lord Jesus—our salvation— saves us!

When we follow Him and allow Him to lead us,
the Lord Jesus—our salvation—saves us.

The Tabernacle of David

There is a prophecy in Amos 9:11 that speaks of our time. It says, "On that day I will raise up the tabernacle of David, which has fallen down, and repair its damages; I will raise up its ruins, and rebuild it as in the days of old." The interesting feature about the tabernacle of David in contrast to the tabernacle of Moses is that it had no veil separating man and God. David could go directly to worship the Lord before the ark of the covenant.

When our Lord Jesus died on the cross and cried out, "It is finished!" (John 19:30), the Bible tells us that at that precise moment "the veil of the temple was torn in two from top to bottom" (Matt. 27:51). God is saying that the way into the Holy of Holies is open! Through Christ, there is no longer any separation between God and man. *Whosoever* believes in Jesus shall never perish. Hallelujah!

David's tabernacle: David and the priests could praise God openly before the ark of the covenant.

Isn't it wonderful to know that when you are in Christ, all your sins are forgiven, that there is no longer a veil that separates you from your Father in heaven, and that you can come boldly to His throne of grace to worship Him? God has raised up the tabernacle of David with a new generation of worshipers who are not afraid of God and not afraid to draw near and receive His promise of divine protection. None of us can ever do enough to merit God's protection, but praise be to God, we are all qualified by the blood of Jesus Christ!

Come boldly to His throne of grace to worship Him and receive His promise of divine protection.

On the night of the first Passover, when the children of Israel applied the blood of an innocent lamb on their doorposts, God said to them, "Now the blood shall be a sign for you on the houses where you *are*. And when I see the blood, I will pass over you; and the plague shall not be on you to destroy *you* when I strike the land of Egypt" (Exod. 12:13). Jesus became that innocent lamb that was sacrificed for us when He shed His blood and died on the cross.

Today, as believers in Christ, His blood protects us. I'm believing with you that all evil, all destruction, and all danger shall pass over you and not come near you and your family. May our confidence be in His blood and not in our own merits to earn God's protection. Today, let us come boldly to worship our Lord in the tabernacle of David where there is no veil. Come boldly under His wings and worship the Lord daily with the prayer of protection. His precious blood has been shed at the mercy seat for our total redemption, protection, and salvation.

Today, as believers in Christ, His blood protects us.

Beloved, I pray that this book has encouraged you to be bold. Psalm 91 was written for worship. Come boldly into our Lord's presence daily and pray the prayer of protection. There is no veil, no failure, and no shame that separates you from God today because of our Lord's finished work at Calvary. Come before your heavenly Father, worship Him, and receive His protection for you and your entire household!

CLOSING WORDS

Over the last twelve chapters, I've endeavored to share with you what the Lord has revealed to me down through the years about the prayer of protection found in Psalm 91. Thank you for staying with me up till now—it has been a tremendous privilege for me to talk to you about the promises of protection that we can stand upon as beloved children of the Most High. I pray that His Word has anchored your heart in faith and cast out every fear as you took this journey with me.

While it's true that we live in dangerous times, I want you to know this: We have our Abba's promise that we can live safe, secure, and protected no matter what turmoil may be around us. Our heavenly Father does not want His children partaking of the fear that has invaded the hearts of people of the world. In fact, He wants *every* trace of fear to be expelled from your heart, knowing that He has set you apart, and that He who watches over you *never* slumbers nor sleeps! When fear comes knocking, let God's promises of protection fill your heart, mind, and mouth, and the God of peace, our *Jehovah Shalom*, will come into and move in your situation!

Our Lord Jesus desires to have an intimate relationship with us and He loves it when we acknowledge our need for Him. He loves it when we allow Him to hide us under the shadow of His wings, close to His heart of love. The prayer of protection is not some magical chant or incantation that grants us protection. Our protection in the Lord is all about us being intimate with and close to Him. As you involve Him in your day-to-day life, you will see Him lead you by His wisdom and protect you from making unwise decisions. And I pray that you will see His protection manifested more and more as you grow in your revelation of how deeply loved you are by the Lord, who protects like no other.

I am so grateful to the precious people who took the time to write to me to share the amazing stories you've read here. I hope these encounters with real people around the world have encouraged you to believe that whatever weapon the enemy may have fashioned against you, it will *not* prosper. God is no respecter of persons—as you keep establishing your heart on the word of grace, as you keep hearing testimonies of His goodness, *you* will also experience miracles of deliverance, protection, and healing in your life.

Today, as you put your trust in the Lord, I pray that you will experience not just His divine protection in a greater measure, but *every* blessing that the Lord Jesus has purchased for you on the cross of Calvary. Beloved, as we garrison our hearts with the truths and promises of Psalm 91, I pray that we will truly live confidently and fearlessly in these dangerous times.

NOTES

CHAPTER 1: *The Secret Place*

1. OT: 3427, James Strong, *Biblesoft's New Exhaustive Strong's Numbers and Concordance with Expanded Greek-Hebrew Dictionary.* Copyright © 1994, 2003, 2006 Biblesoft, Inc. and International Bible Translators, Inc.

CHAPTER 2: *"I Will Say"*

1. OT: 4268, Joseph Henry Thayer, Francis Brown, Samuel Rolles Driver, and Charles Augustus Briggs, *The Online Bible Thayer's Greek Lexicon and Brown Driver & Briggs Hebrew Lexicon.* Copyright © 1993, Woodside Bible Fellowship, Ontario, Canada. Licensed from the Institute for Creation Research.

2. OT: 4686, James Strong, *Biblesoft's New Exhaustive Strong's Numbers and Concordance with Expanded Greek-Hebrew Dictionary.* Copyright © 1994, 2003, 2006 Biblesoft, Inc. and International Bible Translators, Inc.

3. OT: 3068, William Edwy Vine, *Vine's Expository Dictionary of Biblical Words.* Copyright © 1985, Thomas Nelson Publishers.

4. Retrieved March 24, 2016, from www.hebrew-streams.org/frontstuff /jesus-yeshua.html.

5. Retrieved March 24, 2016, from www.hebrew4christians.com /Names_of_G-d/Elohim/elohim.html.

CHAPTER 3: *Right Place, Right Time*

1. Retrieved March 31, 2016, from https://constative.com/history/top-10-richest-men-of-all-time-in.
2. OT: 6256, William Edwy Vine, *Vine's Expository Dictionary of Biblical Words*. Copyright © 1985, Thomas Nelson Publishers.
3. OT: 6293, James Strong, *Biblesoft's New Exhaustive Strong's Numbers and Concordance with Expanded Greek-Hebrew Dictionary*. Copyright © 1994, 2003, 2006 Biblesoft, Inc. and International Bible Translators, Inc.
4. OT: 4745, James Strong, *Biblesoft's New Exhaustive Strong's Numbers and Concordance with Expanded Greek-Hebrew Dictionary*. Copyright © 1994, 2003, 2006 Biblesoft, Inc. and International Bible Translators, Inc.

CHAPTER 4: *Consent to Come Under His Wings*

1. OT: 3727, William Edwy Vine, *Vine's Expository Dictionary of Biblical Words*. Copyright © 1985, Thomas Nelson Publishers.
2. NT: 2799, James Strong, *Biblesoft's New Exhaustive Strong's Numbers and Concordance with Expanded Greek-Hebrew Dictionary*. Copyright © 1994, 2003, 2006 Biblesoft, Inc. and International Bible Translators, Inc.

CHAPTER 5: *Fearless Living*

1. Retrieved March 31, 2016, from www.blueletterbible.org/lang/Lexicon/lexicon.cfm?strongs=H7965&t=KJV.
2. Retrieved April 1, 2016, from http://eresources.nlb.gov.sg/infopedia/articles/SIP_1529_2009-06-03.html.

CHAPTER 7: *Dwell Safely in Christ, Your Refuge*

1. OT: 2620, James Strong, *Biblesoft's New Exhaustive Strong's Numbers and Concordance with Expanded Greek-Hebrew Dictionary*. Copyright © 1994, 2003, 2006 Biblesoft, Inc. and International Bible Translators, Inc.
2. Retrieved April 7, 2016, from www.biblestudytools.com/dictionaries/smiths-bible-dictionary/kedesh.html.

3. Retrieved April 7, 2016, from www.biblestudytools.com/dictionaries /smiths-bible-dictionary/shechem.html.

4. Retrieved April 7, 2016, from http://biblehub.com/topical/h/hebron.htm.

5. OT: 1221, Joseph Henry Thayer, Francis Brown, Samuel Rolles Driver, and Charles Augustus Briggs, *The Online Bible Thayer's Greek Lexicon and Brown Driver & Briggs Hebrew Lexicon*. Copyright © 1993, Wood-side Bible Fellowship, Ontario, Canada. Licensed from the Institute for Creation Research.

6. OT: 7216, Joseph Henry Thayer, Francis Brown, Samuel Rolles Driver, and Charles Augustus Briggs, *The Online Bible Thayer's Greek Lexicon and Brown Driver & Briggs Hebrew Lexicon*. Copyright © 1993, Wood-side Bible Fellowship, Ontario, Canada. Licensed from the Institute for Creation Research.

7. OT: 1474, Joseph Henry Thayer, Francis Brown, Samuel Rolles Driver, and Charles Augustus Briggs, *The Online Bible Thayer's Greek Lexicon and Brown Driver & Briggs Hebrew Lexicon*. Copyright © 1993, Wood-side Bible Fellowship, Ontario, Canada. Licensed from the Institute for Creation Research.

CHAPTER 8: *Activating His Angels*

1. OT: 1870, Joseph Henry Thayer, Francis Brown, Samuel Rolles Driver, and Charles Augustus Briggs, *The Online Bible Thayer's Greek Lexicon and Brown Driver & Briggs Hebrew Lexicon*. Copyright © 1993, Wood-side Bible Fellowship, Ontario, Canada. Licensed from the Institute for Creation Research.

CHAPTER 9: *Time to Play Offense*

1. OT: 7522, Joseph Henry Thayer, Francis Brown, Samuel Rolles Driver, and Charles Augustus Briggs, *The Online Bible Thayer's Greek Lexicon and Brown Driver & Briggs Hebrew Lexicon*. Copyright © 1993, Wood-side Bible Fellowship, Ontario, Canada. Licensed from the Institute for Creation Research.

2. OT: 3722, Joseph Henry Thayer, Francis Brown, Samuel Rolles Driver, and Charles Augustus Briggs, *The Online Bible Thayer's Greek Lexi-con and Brown Driver & Briggs Hebrew Lexicon*. Copyright © 1993,

Woodside Bible Fellowship, Ontario, Canada. Licensed from the Institute for Creation Research.

CHAPTER 10: *Protected by the Father's Love*

1. Retrieved, April 14, 2016, from www.blueletterbible.org/lang/lexicon /lexicon.cfm?t=kjv&strongs=g5083.
2. OT: 1657, Joseph Henry Thayer, Francis Brown, Samuel Rolles Driver, and Charles Augustus Briggs, *The Online Bible Thayer's Greek Lexicon and Brown Driver & Briggs Hebrew Lexicon*. Copyright © 1993, Woodside Bible Fellowship, Ontario, Canada. Licensed from the Institute for Creation Research.

CHAPTER 12: *God's Promise of Long Life*

1. OT: 3444, Joseph Henry Thayer, Francis Brown, Samuel Rolles Driver, and Charles Augustus Briggs, *The Online Bible Thayer's Greek Lexicon and Brown Driver & Briggs Hebrew Lexicon*. Copyright © 1993, Woodside Bible Fellowship, Ontario, Canada. Licensed from the Institute for Creation Research.

SPECIAL APPRECIATION

Special thanks and appreciation to all who have sent in their testimonies and praise reports to us. Kindly note that all testimonies are received in good faith and edited only for brevity and fluency. Names have been changed to protect the writers' privacy.

SALVATION PRAYER

If you would like to receive all that Jesus has done for you and make Him your Lord and Savior, please pray this prayer:

Lord Jesus, thank You for loving me and dying for me on the cross. Your precious blood washes me clean of every sin. You are my Lord and my Savior, now and forever. I believe You rose from the dead and that You are alive today. Because of Your finished work, I am now a beloved child of God and heaven is my home. Thank You for giving me eternal life and filling my heart with Your peace and joy. Amen.

WE WOULD LIKE TO
HEAR FROM YOU

✺

If you have prayed the salvation prayer or if you have a testimony to share after reading this book, please send it to us via JosephPrince.com/testimony.

STAY CONNECTED WITH JOSEPH

Connect with Joseph through these social media channels and receive daily inspirational teachings:

Facebook.com/JosephPrince

Twitter.com/JosephPrince

Youtube.com/JosephPrinceOnline

Instagram: @JosephPrince

FREE DAILY E-MAIL DEVOTIONAL

Sign up for Joseph's FREE daily e-mail devotional at JosephPrince.com/meditate and receive bite-size inspirations to help you grow in grace.

BOOKS BY JOSEPH PRINCE

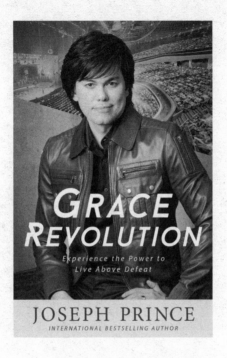

Grace Revolution

Experience the revolution that is sweeping across the world! In *Grace Revolution*, Joseph Prince offers five powerful keys that will help you experience firsthand the grace revolution in your own life, and live above defeat. See how these keys can work easily for you, as you read inspiring stories of people who experienced amazing and lasting transformations when they encountered the real Jesus and heard the unadulterated gospel. Whatever your challenge today, begin to step away from defeat and take a massive leap toward your victory. Get your copy today and let the revolution begin in your life!

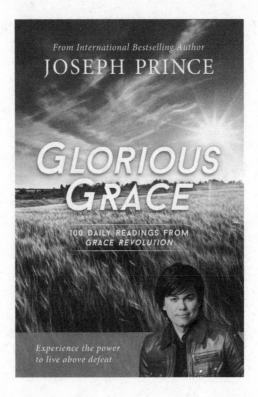

Glorious Grace

Experience the grace revolution firsthand today! Through one hundred powerful, bite-size daily inspirations, step out of hopelessness and defeat into a life of boldness, peace, and power. Taking key teachings from *Grace Revolution*, each daily reading offers a faith-fueling Scripture to anchor your heart on the certainty of God's love toward you, as well as a key truth and liberating thought of the day on His amazing grace that will usher in His peace and restoration into your life. Let these faith-building devotionals take you on a powerful journey of experiencing God's glorious grace in your life today.

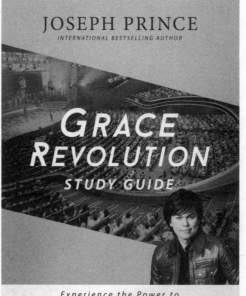

Experience the Power to
Live Above Defeat

Grace Revolution Study Guide

Establish yourself in the gospel of grace through this *Grace Revolution Study Guide*, and begin to experience the lasting breakthroughs you seek! Each chapter has carefully selected gospel truths from *Grace Revolution*, as well as pertinent questions that will deepen your understanding of the true gospel and ignite hope and confidence in God's love for you to overcome your challenges. Whether you use this study guide on your own or with a group, you'll find each session exciting and rewarding. As you grow in the knowledge of the Lord Jesus and His grace through this study guide, you'll find His Spirit transforming and leading you to victory!

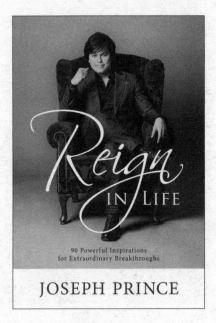

Reign in Life

Through ninety powerful inspirations that help you discover God's transforming grace, unleash His liberty and power to reign in all areas of life! When you reign, sin, sicknesses, addictions, and bondages don't. When you reign, God's provision, healing, wholeness, favor, and abundant life begin to manifest in your life. Let the truths of God's grace and the inspiring, personal stories of precious people transformed by His grace lead you to embark on your own journey of experiencing extraordinary breakthroughs.

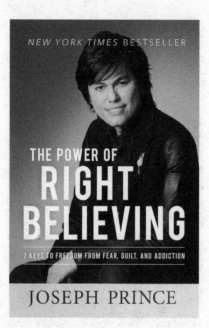

The Power of Right Believing

Experience transformation, breakthroughs, and freedom today through the power of right believing! This book offers seven practical and powerful keys that will help you find freedom from all fears, guilt, and addictions. See these keys come alive in the many precious testimonies you will read from people around the world who have experienced breakthroughs and liberty from all kinds of bondages. Win the battle for your mind through understanding the powerful truths of God's Word and begin a journey of victorious living and unshakable confidence in God's love for you!

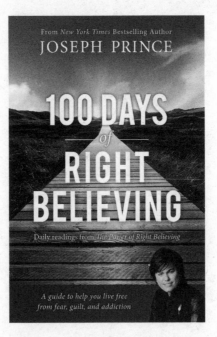

100 Days of Right Believing

What you believe is everything! When you begin to believe right, the breakthroughs you want to see in your life will manifest. With key teachings from *The Power of Right Believing*, this hundred-day devotional aims to help you develop highly effective habits for right believing that will set you free from fears, guilt, addictions, and all kinds of bondages. With faith-building Scriptures, prayers, and powerful thoughts, these inspiring devotionals will lead you to encounter God's love and grace afresh each day and liberate you to live a life of joy and victory.

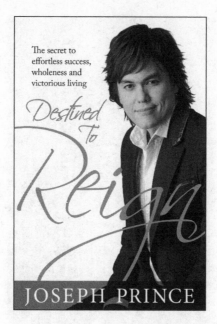

Destined To Reign

This pivotal and quintessential book on the grace of God will change your life forever! Join Joseph Prince as he unlocks foundational truths to understanding God's grace and how it alone sets you free to experience victory over every adversity, lack, and destructive habit that is limiting you today. Be uplifted and refreshed as you discover how reigning in life is all about Jesus and what He has already done for you. Start experiencing the success, wholeness, and victory that you were destined to enjoy!

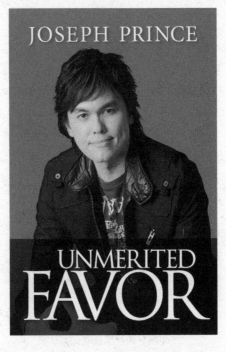

Unmerited Favor

This follow-up book to *Destined To Reign* is a must-read if you want to live out the dreams that God has birthed in your heart! Building on the foundational truths of God's grace laid out in *Destined To Reign*, *Unmerited Favor* takes you into a deeper understanding of the gift of righteousness that you have through the cross and how it gives you a supernatural ability to succeed in life. Packed with empowering new covenant truths, *Unmerited Favor* will set you free to soar above your challenges and lead an overcoming life as God's beloved today.

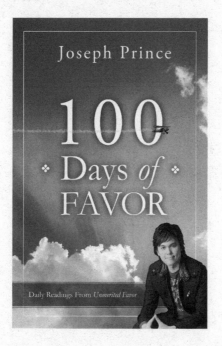

100 Days of Favor

Dive headfirst into the vast ocean of God's favor and learn how it releases success in your life! Taking key teachings from *Unmerited Favor* and turning them into bite-size daily devotionals, Joseph Prince shows you how to develop favor-consciousness that releases the wisdom and blessings of God in everything you do, every day. With inspirational Scriptures, prayers, and liberating thoughts on God's unmerited favor in each devotional, *100 Days of Favor* is a must-have resource that will empower you to overcome every challenge in your life and walk in success.